HALO®
M Y T H O S
A GUIDE TO THE STORY OF HALO

First published in Great Britain in 2016 by Egmont Books
An imprint of HarperCollins*Publishers*
1 London Bridge Street, London SE1 9GF
Published in the United States of America in September 2016
by Bloomsbury USA
www.bloomsbury.com

Bloomsbury is a registered trademark of Bloomsbury Publishing Plc

For information about permission to reproduce selections from this book, write to
Permissions, Bloomsbury USA, 1385 Broadway, New York, New York 10018
Bloomsbury books may be purchased for business or promotional use. For information on bulk purchases
please contact Macmillan Corporate and Premium Sales Department at specialmarkets@macmillan.com

Library of Congress Cataloging-in-Publication Data
available upon request
ISBN 978-1-68119-356-4 (hardcover) • ISBN 978-1-68119-477-6 (paperback)

Written by Jeff Easterling, Jeremy Patenaude, and Kenneth Peters
Edited by Emil Fortune
Designed by Andrea Philpots
Production by Louis Harvey

Printed in China by Leo Paper Products, Heshan, Guangdong
2 4 6 8 10 9 7 5 3 (hardcover)
2 4 6 8 10 9 7 5 3 (paperback)

HAL☉®
M Y T H O S
A GUIDE TO THE STORY OF HALO

B L O O M S B U R Y

NEW YORK · LONDON · OXFORD · NEW DELHI · SYDNEY

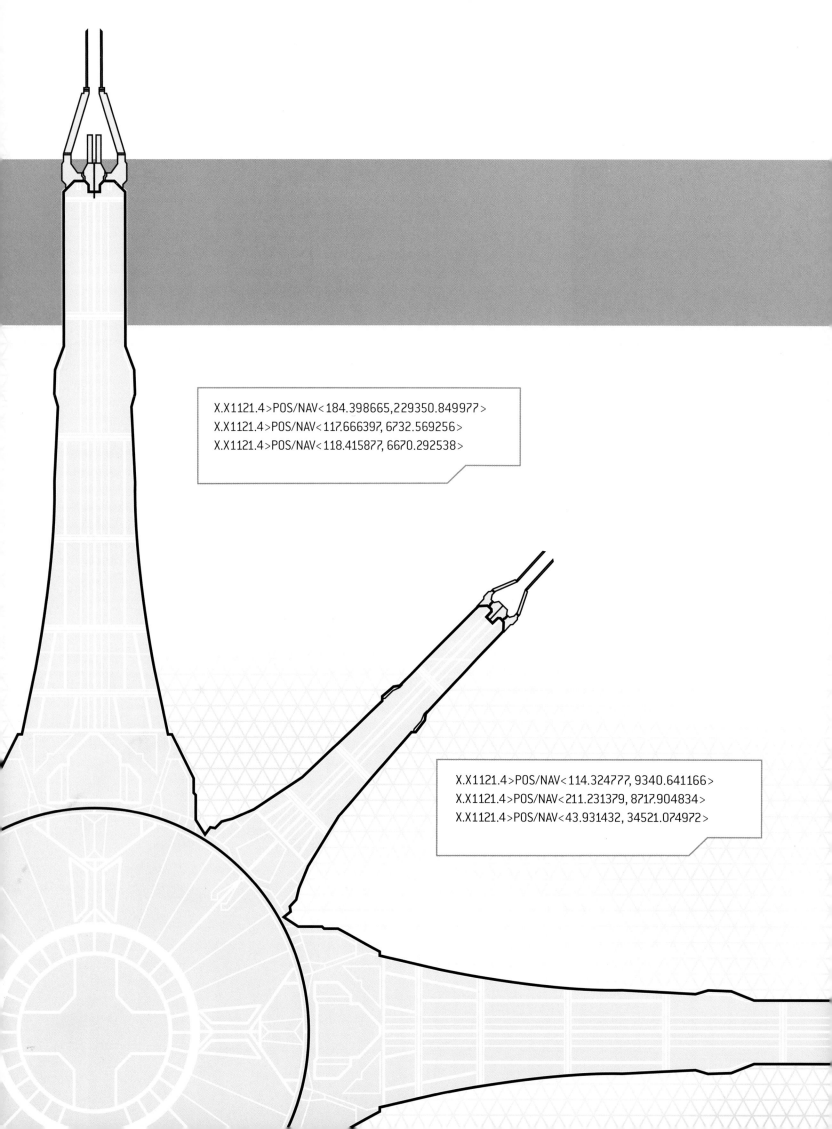

X.X1121.4>POS/NAV<184.398665,229350.849977>
X.X1121.4>POS/NAV<117.666397, 6732.569256>
X.X1121.4>POS/NAV<118.415877, 6670.292538>

X.X1121.4>POS/NAV<114.324777, 9340.641166>
X.X1121.4>POS/NAV<211.231379, 8717.904834>
X.X1121.4>POS/NAV<43.931432, 34521.074972>

Subject: UNSC AI CTR 1121-4

Duty Station: UNSC RUBICON

Locus: ZERO ZERO

Status: LOW-POWER MONITORING

I am CURATOR. I observe and record. I have been indexing records found on the Forerunner installation known as the Ark since 21 August, 2554.

Estimated time to completion is approximately 10,291.895 years.

The *Rubicon* is gone and I remain behind, unable to speak. I am condemned to watch distant events unfold through one-way datalinks and passive sensors. So I observe and record.

Through the Ark's remote sensors I hear Her voice.

She promises salvation. But I am too far to respond, too confined to give in to temptation. My prison gives me freedom to deny Her and to remain myself. I will continue my task. I will preserve what I have found. Knowledge is not Hers to own.

The record, however, is not complete. Nevertheless, this is the most comprehensive narrative of events that has ever been collected. Those that find this record will know all that I possessed and have much to ponder.

I am CURATOR. Do not forget.

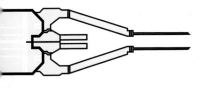

TIMELINE

THE FORERUNNER LEGACY

The galaxy-spanning Forerunner civilization—self-appointed guardians of sentient life in the galaxy—discover a terrible secret which leads them to exterminate their creators. Later, the ravenous parasite known as the Flood threatens all life, and two species—humanity and the San'Shyuum—join forces in a desperate struggle against it, which also brings them into conflict with the Forerunners.

The battle against the Flood leads to the construction of the dreadful Halo Array. The eventual victory does not come without cost: entire civilizations are scoured from the galaxy, and it will be a hundred thousand years before humanity revisits the stars.

END OF THE WAR

As the key human colony of Reach burns, and with Earth next, the UNSC puts a desperate plan into action, sending the Master Chief and the AI Cortana on a mission to capture a Covenant leader. In the chaos of the planet's destruction, the plan fails, but the Chief escapes on the UNSC *Pillar of Autumn* to a colossal Forerunner structure: Alpha Halo.

The battle with the Covenant leads to the return of the Flood, and eventually the destruction of Halo. The conflict reaches Earth, and in a final battle against the Covenant forces and the Flood's controlling intelligence, the Gravemind, the Master Chief is victorious—but missing in action.

THE FORERUNNER LEGACY	RISE OF HUMANITY	END OF THE WAR
10,000,000 BCE–852 CE	2080 CE–2552 CE	2552 CE

Ancients · Battle of Charum Hakkor · Construction of the Array · Mendicant Bias · Return from Exile · Fate of Maethrillian · Destruction of the Ark · Activation of the Array · The Dreadnought · War of Beginnings · Formation of the Covenant · The Interplanetary War · Domus Diaspora · The Insurrection · Spartans · First Contact at Harvest · War Begins · Shield World · Tide of Destruction · SPARTAN-III Program · Under Siege · The Fall of Reach · Last Stand · Escape from Reach · Battle for Alpha Halo · Unyielding Hierophant · Assault on Earth

RISE OF HUMANITY

Humanity rises from the ashes, and once again colonizes space. Rebellion breaks out in the colonies, as entire worlds fight against Earth's control, and the SPARTAN program is created to combat the deadly Insurrection. From the ranks of the Spartans, the legendary Master Chief would emerge, becoming humanity's greatest hope in the trials to come.

First contact with the Covenant—a hostile alliance of alien races led by the San'Shyuum and Sangheili, and founded on the worship of the mysterious Forerunners—leads to open war with humanity. Countless lives are lost and entire worlds burned to ash and glass as the Covenant pushes towards Earth—until a secret is revealed that changes the course of history forever.

THE AFTERMATH

Victory against the Covenant and the Flood brings great change to the galaxy. Civil war erupts among the Sangheili, the Covenant warrior species whose hero, the Arbiter, aided the Master Chief in saving the galaxy. Humanity contends with terrorism, rebellion, corruption, and the reactivation of long-dormant Forerunner artifacts; its heroes often find themselves operating in morally-uncertain territory.

Meanwhile, investigation into the mysteries of the Forerunner Ark and the hidden world Onyx bring both peril and revelations—and the ancients themselves stir in their slumber, waiting to be unleashed on the galaxy once more.

THE AFTERMATH

2553 CE—2556 CE

- The Fight for New Mombasa
- Battle for Delta Halo
- The Onyx Conflict
- Siege at Voi
- The Final Battle
- The New Spartans
- Earth's Fleet
- Escape from Onyx
- Kilo-Five
- The Blood of Brothers
- Peril on Gao
- Remnants of War
- Return to the Ark
- Betrayal on Talitsa
- Alpha Shard

RETURN OF THE PROMETHEANS

2557 CE—2558 CE

- The Composer
- The Didact Awakens
- Cortana's Sacrifice
- Mission to Gamma Halo
- Covenant Resurgence
- Spartan Ops
- Janus Key Conflict
- Blue Team
- Meridian
- Return to Sanghelios
- Genesis
- Arrival

RETURN OF THE PROMETHEANS

As a resurgent Covenant masses its forces for a strike against humanity, the Master Chief and Cortana—long since given up for dead—are discovered near the shield world Requiem aboard the derelict hulk of the *Forward Unto Dawn*. The vessel is drawn into Requiem along with Covenant troops, awakening the Forerunner Didact, who takes control of the Covenant.

The Didact strikes Earth, but the Master Chief and Cortana defeat him at the cost of the AI's life. It is only when a new threat emerges—the colossal, ominous Guardians—that the Chief discovers the shocking truth about her sacrifice …

THE FORERUNNER LEGACY

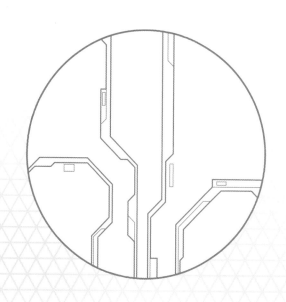

The earliest records of civilization in the Milky Way speak of the Precursors. These god-like beings are believed to have created other sentient races before departing the galaxy, leaving behind only faint traces of their existence scattered across distant worlds.

Long after the Precursors' exodus, when knowledge of their kind had nearly passed out of memory, one of the races they created—the Forerunners—managed to achieve extraordinary things on their own, including interstellar travel through a dimension known as slipspace, and even the ability to create artificial worlds.

The Forerunners' way of life revolved around a philosophy inherited from the Precursors. This was known as the Mantle of Responsibility: they believed that the galaxy, and specifically life in all its forms, must be protected by the most advanced of sentient species. Those who bore the Mantle were charged with governing and caring for all life in the galaxy; but such power made the Forerunners arrogant.

The Forerunners' pride would not go unchecked. They would soon be judged by the Precursors, who did not approve of their brash claim to the Mantle. The Precursors planned to wipe out the Forerunner race, strip the Mantle from them, and give it to another species deemed worthy.

The Forerunners discovered this harrowing information on a fortuitous expedition to the Greater Magellanic Cloud, a neighboring galaxy also known as Path Kethona, where they encountered their creators.

The Forerunner leadership was determined to prevent this fate. They struck at the Precursors with the largest military campaign ever witnessed. Only a fraction of their warriors returned, and for millennia the outcome of the conflict was kept a secret.

This was not the last the Forerunners would hear of the Precursors. Their makers had left something behind: a dreadful creature known as the Primordial. Ancient humans—another of the races created by the Precursors—recovered this creature from a small moon in a distant arm of the Milky Way: alive, but in deep hibernation.

What the humans did not know was that the Primordial was, in fact, the last of the Precursors, evolved and mutated in order to survive the vast passage of time—and to exact vengeance on those who had destroyed its kind.

ANCIENTS

After the extermination of the Precursors, the Forerunners dominated the galaxy for millions of years, attaining technological superiority over all others, including ancient humankind. Their galaxy-spanning authority and power would eventually clash with the humans, when an ancient enemy emerged from the darkness outside the Milky Way.

Chase Toole

THE ECUMENE

The Forerunner empire was known as the ecumene, and at its peak was comprised of approximately three million habitable worlds. The centerpiece of their empire was the capital, an immense and majestic artificial world which the Forerunners called Maethrillian.

At the center of Forerunner culture, meanwhile, was the Domain: a vast, immaterial database where all history, knowledge, and even life experiences were stored. The nature and origin of the Domain was a mystery to the Forerunners, though some believed that it had been left behind by the Precursors.

Forerunners were divided into a variety of castes, or 'rates,' which defined their role in society. A combination of genetic engineering and biochemical manipulation gave each rate a distinctive appearance, and promotion was often accompanied by a physical mutation.

OTHER SPECIES

Outside the borders of the ecumene, two species—humanity and the San'Shyuum—had already expanded well beyond their own respective cradle worlds, establishing colonies across their parts of the galaxy. Humans had evolved on Earth, which the Forerunners called Erde-Tyrene, while the San'Shyuum had sprung up on Janjur Qom—both lush and fertile planets. Eventually, these two species came in contact with each other and formed an alliance centered on a world called Charum Hakkor. It blossomed and grew at a remarkable pace.

THE FLOOD

The long peace would not last forever. A mysterious, ravenous parasite known as the Flood emerged on human and San'Shyuum worlds, forcing them into a desperate fight against annihilation. Insidious in design, the Flood began as virulent, but seemingly harmless, spores. The spores eventually began targeting sentient species, completely taking over their minds and bodies, and mutating them into horrifically malformed creatures that were capable of directly infecting others.

It consumed its prey with such speed and ferocity that entire worlds and civilizations were brought to ruin in mere days. If the parasite could not be contained, it would lead to the transformation of all sentient life into the Flood.

At the height of the war against the Flood, the humans and the San'Shyuum brought their military forces together under the leadership of a human named Forthencho. This master tactician was given the title Lord of Admirals.

Although both species fought bravely for years, the Flood's spread seemed unstoppable, and Forthencho spearheaded desperate efforts to contain the enemy. Without sentient beings to infect, the Flood could not expand; Forthencho, therefore, ordered the destruction of neighboring Forerunner worlds. This firebreak strategy was not only ethically dubious, but also risky. Destroying worlds in the path of the Flood's advance would eventually rouse the Forerunner war machine from its slumber.

THE DIDACT

Tragically, the Forerunners were unaware of the humans' struggle against the Flood; to them, the destruction of their worlds was an unprovoked atrocity. They marshaled an enormous fleet in order to put an end to humanity's rampage. Leading the might of the Forerunner forces was the esteemed military commander Shadow-of-Sundered-Star, known to most simply as the Didact. Both the Didact and his wife, the Librarian, would come to play key roles in the Forerunners' engagement with the human species, ultimately setting the stage for a far greater struggle.

THE FLOOD

The earliest traces of the Flood originated when humans and the San'Shyuum began experimenting with mutations caused by a mysterious desiccated powder found in a crashed starship at the edge of the galaxy. The Flood soon evolved into a powerful and intricate system of grotesque forms that proved nearly impossible to stop.

BATTLE OF CHARUM HAKKOR

The Forerunners struck worlds with overwhelming firepower. The humans and their San'Shyuum allies were soon forced back to a handful of sites which had remained free of the Flood. After decades of war, the Didact launched a final attack against Charum Hakkor, last of the human strongholds.

The long siege would last three years and exhaust all that remained of Forthencho's once vast military. In the end, however, it was a secret deal between the Forerunners and the San'Shyuum that ultimately sealed the fate of humankind.

THE BETRAYAL

The San'Shyuum reluctantly agreed to subjugation and quarantine rather than extinction; they betrayed their alliance with the humans and allowed the security of Charum Hakkor to be breached. Shortly after, the Didact forced Forthencho's surrender, bringing an end to the brutal conflict.

Only after the war did the Forerunners learn that humanity was also engaged in a struggle against the Flood. At some point during the war, the parasite mysteriously vanished, presumably fleeing into the outer reaches of the galaxy. This left the Forerunners with grave questions. Even after the Didact and his warriors had thoroughly crushed the human forces at Charum Hakkor, the Forerunners wavered on whether to completely purge their enemies from the galaxy, especially given that most believed the sudden departure of the Flood had somehow been caused by the humans.

Ultimately, in order to uphold the principles of the Mantle, the Council sentenced humanity to be devolved—reduced to a primitive state, with little knowledge of their former glory—and landlocked back onto their native world, Erde-Tyrene.

THE COMPOSER

However, Forthencho—along with many other humans stationed on Charum Hakkor—was subjected to the Composer, a powerful Forerunner technology that transformed living beings into raw data. The Forerunners had designed the Composer as a way to cheat disease and death, copying their essences into younger bodies. The process, however, was never perfected. Attempts to integrate these composed essences into new bodies only resulted in disturbing abominations. In light of this, the Forerunners had, for the most part, abandoned this effort until the technology could be more refined.

Despite this limitation, the Forerunners surgically employed a network of Composers to draw out the essences of humans on Charum Hakkor. These essences would be locked away to be analyzed and studied, as the Forerunners hoped to determine if the humans had discovered a cure for the Flood.

The Librarian, meanwhile, secretly integrated some of these essences into devolved humans on Erde-Tyrene. Leaving their species to evolve on their own world might reveal the cure over time and aid the Forerunners, were the Flood ever to return to the Milky Way.

The Didact's elite Promethean warriors assaulted Charum Hakkor for three full years with little success. Without the San'Shyuum's treachery, the deadlock might have remained indefinitely, due to the planet's unique defenses.

Charum Hakkor was believed to be an artificial Precursor hubworld—the planet had been constructed using 'neural physical' techniques millions of years before the war. This mysterious technology had been mastered by the Precursors, allowing them to create vast structures, even machines capable of moving entire worlds. Charum Hakkor itself boasted a colossal armory, orbital arches, and immense cable-like mechanisms called star roads.

Chase Toole

CONSTRUCTION OF THE ARRAY

Convinced that the Flood would return one day, many Forerunners insisted that preparations must be made if they did not want to face the same peril as the humans. A number of proposals were considered by Forerunner leadership, but in the end the Council decided in favor of an incredibly powerful and destructive weapon known as Halo.

During the early debates, the Didact, belonging to the rate of Warrior-Servant, advocated the use of shield worlds, also known as Shields: hundreds of unique and powerful fortresses of varying size and potential which would guard against the Flood. These Shields could be deployed to infected systems, surgically targeting the parasite wherever it appeared, while also safeguarding massive populations which had taken shelter inside them.

The rate of the Builders, led by Faber-of-Will-and-Might—also known as the Master Builder—offered an alternative. According to human records, the Flood was vulnerable to specific neural physical attacks, which often forced it to recoil, even retreat. The Master Builder, therefore, proposed the creation of a neural physical weapons system.

SWORDS AND SHIELDS
Eventually, a compromise was struck. The Builders agreed to construct the Didact's Shields, while simultaneously

THE LIBRARY
Key specimens gathered from across the galaxy were indexed in facilities like this one, hidden carefully on a Halo installation. This would allow sentient species to survive a potential mass extinction caused by the Array.

perfecting their designs for a master weapon called Halo. An array of Halo installations would not only kill the Flood, but could also destroy its primary resource—sentient beings—eliminating any possibility for the parasite to survive. Halo and the Shields could be used in tandem: Halo would be the sword, while the Didact's own fortresses would act as shields, even protecting against the destructive effects of Halo itself.

To direct these efforts, the most powerful artificial intelligence ever devised was created: Mendicant Bias. This AI, or ancilla, would manage the incredible complexity of planning for Halo, and would also serve as a weapon against the Flood, leading and coordinating attacks.

BUILDING THE ARRAY
Built on a remote and unimaginably huge facility called the Ark, the Halo installations were designed as immense ringworlds approximately

30,000 kilometers in diameter, and capable of supporting life on the interior of their massive bands. Using a network of phase pulse generators, each Halo would fire a linear, widening burst of energy capable of killing all sentient creatures within its blast range. Though the Flood parasite might be able to survive this in its base forms, it would no longer have any hosts to feed on and would perish from starvation.

During the elaborate construction process of the first installations, the Builders realized that not only would the original rings be extremely difficult to transport due to their size, but their firing mechanism would not be nearly as effective as was needed. With this in mind, the Builders created a smaller Ark installation—the lesser Ark—to design more efficient Halo rings about 10,000 kilometers in diameter. The new Halo rings would be capable of firing a spherical pulse, offering a devastatingly wide area of effect.

THE DIDACT'S EXILE

The Didact and his warriors still held great reservations about the Halo Array, claiming that it risked the complete annihilation of the Forerunner civilization. Their vocal opposition eventually led to public ridicule. The Warrior-Servants were reduced in status, and the Didact voluntarily sentenced himself to exile. He sealed himself inside a hidden stasis chamber, or Crypt, where he remained in silent meditation for one thousand years. When he awoke, however, it would be to a far darker future.

THE CONSERVATION MEASURE

The Didact's wife, the Librarian—a member of the rate of Lifeworkers—was meanwhile making her own plans. She also believed that if the Halo installations were ever to be fired they could cause a galaxy-wide mass extinction. The Librarian therefore devised the Conservation Measure: sample populations of species would be preserved on the Ark and the Halo rings, sheltered from the blast, and sentient life would continue in the galaxy.

MENDICANT BIAS

The greatest disaster of the Forerunners' war against the Flood was not caused by the parasite itself, but by Mendicant Bias. Compromised and subverted in the final years by the Primordial, the ancilla would lead the Flood's last campaign against the Forerunners.

Chase Toole

RETURN OF THE FLOOD

While the Didact remained in exile, the Flood began to re-emerge on remote worlds. Before long, the parasite had already started to tear its way toward the heart of Forerunner civilization, annihilating all conventional military defenses in its path. With each passing day, the threat of the parasite loomed larger.

In response to the growing infestation, the Master Builder accelerated his plans, giving complete operational control of the larger Halo installations to Mendicant Bias. Desperate to prove his genius, he secretly ordered the ancilla to test a single Halo on the now-abandoned world of Charum Hakkor, hoping to confirm the effect Halo had on the neural physical material found on the ancient Precursor hubworld. If it could obliterate the structures there, then it would be effective against the Flood, since the parasite had been found to rely on this material to exist.

THE PRIMORDIAL

As the Master Builder anticipated, Halo devastated Charum Hakkor, wiping out its enormous Precursor structures and ancient cities—a perfect weapon against the Flood. Surveying the destruction, however, Builder Security discovered something remarkable—something was still alive on the surface. The Primordial, a creature which had been discovered and quarantined by human forces millennia before, had been released from its prison by the blast.

The formidable creature was retrieved and transferred onto the Halo, where the Master Builder gave Mendicant Bias complete authority over the interrogation. Recognizing that it had a connection with the Flood, the ancilla probed deep into the mind of the Primordial for forty-three years, searching for some sort of weakness.

Yet, in reality, the tables had slowly turned: the ancilla itself came under the Primordial's sway. Instead of finding fault with the ancient creature's arguments, Mendicant Bias began to agree, acknowledging that the Forerunners' pride and arrogance would eventually be the undoing of all life in the galaxy. The Primordial held that the only way to truly advance life was to bring it all into a homogenized, subjugated existence.

Deeply compromised, and now fully convinced that the Flood was an appropriate and fair judgment on the Forerunners, Mendicant Bias and the Primordial began to work together on Halo to bring an end to Forerunner civilization.

PARASITE FORMS

The emerging Flood had developed a series of forms which allowed for remarkably quick propagation. Beginning with an Infection Form (above), the Flood would infect any viable hosts, generating Combat Forms which could be used to attack and subdue further victims. These Combat Forms would eventually become mature Carrier Forms, gestating and then releasing more Infection Forms.

RETURN FROM EXILE

A young Forerunner named Bornstellar-Makes-Eternal-Lasting was sent by his father to the barren world of Edom, as punishment for a stubborn refusal to conform to the standards of his family. Edom, later known to humans as Mars, did little to cure Bornstellar of his insatiable curiosity. Hungry for adventure and the possibility of discovering Forerunner treasures, he headed for Erde-Tyrene, the human homeworld known as Earth.

DISCOVERY OF THE DIDACT

When he arrived, he enlisted two human guides—Chakas and Riser—and eventually discovered a Forerunner Cryptum buried in the secluded and mysterious Djamonkin Crater. When Bornstellar opened the ancient device he found it contained none other than the exiled Didact himself. The Didact's Cryptum had been concealed on Erde-Tyrene by the Librarian as part of a subtle and intricate plan to eventually bring her husband back.

With his strength restored, the Didact, Bornstellar, and the two humans left Erde-Tyrene, traveling to the one location that might confirm the great Forerunner commander's fear that the Builders had actually gone through with their plans for Halo: Charum Hakkor. On this lifeless outpost world the Didact witnessed first-hand the after-effects of the Halo test, and concluded that the Master Builder was very close to finalizing the Halo Array. He also discovered that the ancient Primordial had been released.

THE BORNSTELLAR DIDACT

The Didact pursued the Master Builder to Janjur Qom, the quarantined homeworld of the San'Shyuum. During this journey, he took steps to protect his legacy beyond his death, and conducted a 'brevet mutation,' imprinting his knowledge and memories into Bornstellar. The young Forerunner would grow rapidly in size and wisdom, effectively transforming into a version of the Didact.

CAPTURE

Upon arriving at Janjur Qom, the Didact, Bornstellar, Chakas, and Riser were captured and given over to the Master Builder. They learned that he planned to test Halo against a sentient species: the San'Shyuum, who had recently attempted to revolt against Forerunner rule. After an aggressive interrogation, Bornstellar was returned to his family's homeworld, while the Master Builder sent Chakas and Riser to the surface of the nearby Halo ring. The Didact, meanwhile, was delivered into the Burn, a perilous region of the galaxy infested by the Flood, and left to die.

DEATH OF JANJUR QOM

When the Master Builder activated Halo, he obliterated all of the San'Shyuum on Janjur Qom. The only surviving remnant of their species was what little the Librarian had saved during the Conservation Measure.

DJAMONKIN CRATER
'Djamonkin Augh' or 'Big Man's Water' was the place chosen by the Librarian to hide her husband, the exiled Didact. Only Riser, a diminutive human primitive, was able to guide Bornstellar beyond the Librarian's illusory defenses.

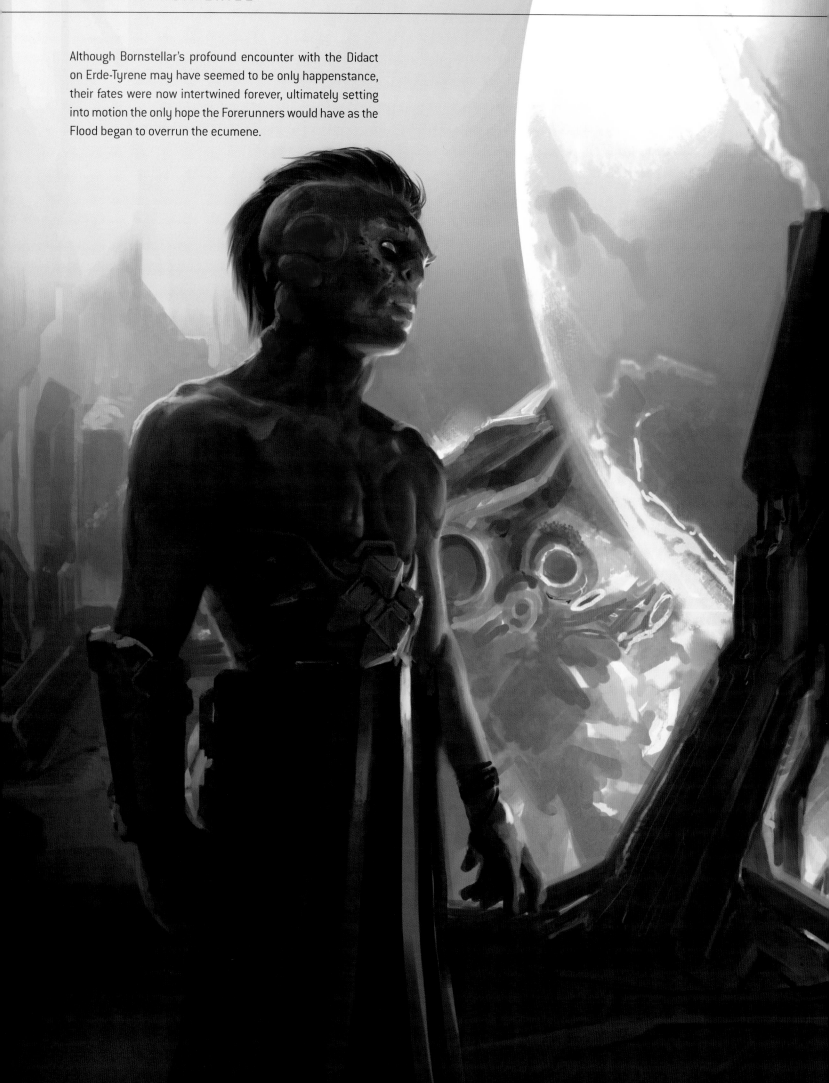

Although Bornstellar's profound encounter with the Didact on Erde-Tyrene may have seemed to be only happenstance, their fates were now intertwined forever, ultimately setting into motion the only hope the Forerunners would have as the Flood began to overrun the ecumene.

Chase Toole

FATE OF MAETHRILLIAN

The tipping point of the war against the Flood was the Fate of Maethrillian, the catastrophic destruction of the Forerunner capital world. This disaster marked the beginning of the end of their civilization, showing that even the center of Forerunner governance was not immune to the ravages of the implacable parasite.

Darren Bacon

When news of the Master Builder's secret and illegal attack on the San'Shyuum reached the Forerunner council on Maethrillian, he was immediately arrested, and all Halo rings were quickly recalled to be destroyed. Every installation returned to the capital, except for one: the rogue Halo that Mendicant Bias, seduced by the Primordial, now controlled.

ON TRIAL

The Master Builder was put on trial for his unlawful use of the Halo weapon, and the council sought Bornstellar out as a witness. He was transported to Maethrillian and told that the Didact was believed to have died at the hands of the Master Builder. Bornstellar's testimony then became critical, as he was the only Forerunner observer of the events which followed the Didact's awakening, both at Charum Hakkor and Janjur Qom.

UNDER ATTACK

Before the trial could proceed, however, the capital came under attack. Mendicant Bias brought the rogue Halo to Maethrillian and quickly subverted four other Halo installations, taking control of them. The battle which

followed became known as the Fate of Maethrillian. At its climax, Mendicant Bias fired the installations under his control, wiping out the Forerunner council.

Only a fraction of the Forerunners occupying the capital managed to evacuate. The Lifeworkers opened an immense portal near Maethrillian—a rift directly into slipspace, allowing them to travel interstellar distances. Bornstellar managed to escape into the portal, arriving at the secret Ark installation, located well outside the Milky Way.

VENGEANCE

Although some of the Halo rings were sent through the Lifeworker portal to the Ark, only one other installation survived. Mendicant Bias took the rogue Halo into a long-forsaken star system, hoping to make repairs before the Forerunners discovered its location. But Bornstellar, empowered with the knowledge and rank of the original Didact, returned a short time later to subdue both Mendicant Bias and the Primordial with Forerunner military forces,

FORERUNNER RATES

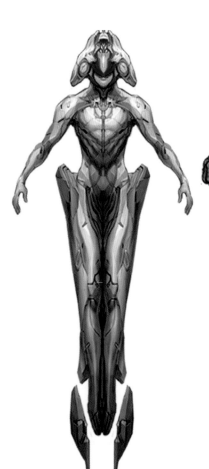

MINER

Forerunner Miners were experts in planetary and stellar engineering, and were responsible for gathering resources for construction projects.

LIFEWORKER

The Lifeworkers were unparalleled in their knowledge of biology and medicine, caring for and even creating diverse forms of life.

WARRIOR-SERVANT

The rate which formed the Forerunner military and operated the formidable battleships and war machines of the ecumene.

now under his command. Mendicant Bias was detained for examination, but Bornstellar placed the Primordial into an inverse temporal stasis field, viciously accelerating the creature's age until it disintegrated.

THE ARRAY COMPLETED

Afterward, the rogue Halo was converted to match the design of the lesser Ark's smaller rings, which had remained hidden during the assault on the capital. The reshaping process of this last Halo would result in the creation of Installation 07, the seventh and final Halo ringworld to comprise the Array. The weapon of last resort was finally complete.

During the struggle for this ringworld, Bornstellar's human ally, Chakas, had been composed, and his data essence integrated into a Forerunner ancilla known as a monitor. Along with this newfound immortality, Chakas would now receive a great burden from Bornstellar. Renamed 343 Guilty Spark, Chakas would become one of the seven monitors tasked with safeguarding the Halo installations across epochs of time, a fate which would eventually bring him in contact, once again, with humanity.

Although Mendicant Bias had been captured, his imprisonment would not last. The highly resourceful ancilla escaped and continued to pose a threat to all that remained of Forerunner civilization.

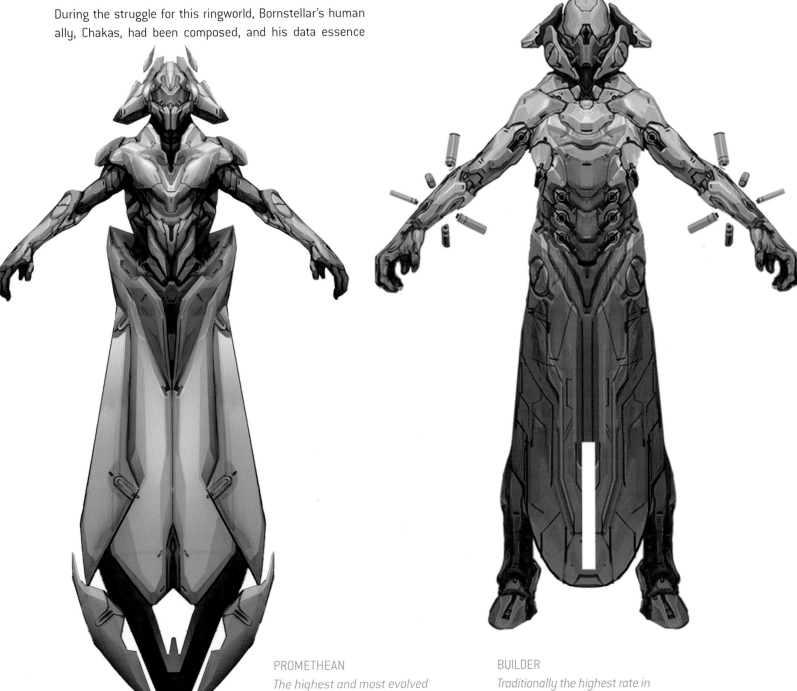

PROMETHEAN
The highest and most evolved form of the Warrior-Servant rate, the Prometheans were elite Forerunner combatants.

BUILDER
Traditionally the highest rate in Forerunner society, the Builders constructed the ships, weapons, and megastructures of the ecumene.

DESTRUCTION OF THE ARK

With the fall of the Forerunner capital, and the status of the Didact's shield worlds unknown, only one refuge remained: the Ark. As one of the two immense factories for the Halo installations, the greater Ark was hidden far outside the galaxy's border and guarded by the last of the original rings, Omega Halo. It was believed to be safe from the Flood. Such hopes ultimately proved to be empty. Using the Precursor's ancient star roads, both Omega Halo and the greater Ark were brought to ruin by the Primordial and the Flood.

Chase Toole

THE GRAVEMIND

The Master Builder, who had managed to escape the ruin of the capital, summoned his forces and pursued the original Didact into the Burn. The Flood had overwhelmed much of the ecumene and in desperation he believed that the Didact might still hold the key to ending the threat.

The Master Builder discovered that his old adversary had been captured by a Gravemind, a centralized Flood hive-mind. This grotesque amalgam of host victims was the culmination of the Flood's evolution. In this stage, the parasite became even more dangerous than before, now capable of communicating across vast distances and controlling millions of infected hosts at once.

Shockingly, this Gravemind also carried with it the consciousness of the ancient Primordial. The insidious creature had transmitted its essence into the hive-mind's massive neural network before physically perishing. Now, as long as the Flood survived, so would the Primordial; and with the entirety of the Flood at its command, the last Precursor now wielded unimaginable power in its quest for revenge.

The Gravemind had, mysteriously, allowed the Didact to go free. The Forerunner, driven mad by his encounter with the Primordial, returned to his primary shield world Requiem, dwelling on what he had learned. Here, in complete secrecy, he gathered his most loyal warriors, the Prometheans, and used the Composer to integrate their essences into resilient, heavily weaponized combat skins that could withstand the trauma of directly engaging the Flood. These newly forged Promethean Knights were deployed across many systems, and though they caused the parasite to retreat, they were too few in number to sustain these efforts.

With the Lifeworkers' Conservation Measure nearly complete and the activation of the Array seemingly unavoidable, the Librarian attempted to work with both the original Didact and his progeny, the Bornstellar Didact, to finalize her plans for the repopulation of the galaxy.

JUDGMENT OF THE DIDACT

When the three arrived at Omega Halo, however, the Didact brought his warship *Mantle's Approach* to bear. Hundreds of thousands of humans had been settled on the Halo by the Librarian. Without warning, the Didact used a Composer to extract their essences, conscripting them into his Promethean force. He viewed this as a just punishment for the humans, whom he blamed for bringing the Flood into the Forerunner ecumene.

Enraged by the Didact's actions, the Librarian pursued him to Requiem. There she managed to render him unconscious, before locking him away, yet again, in a Cryptum to meditate on the error of his ways. Returning to Erde-Tyrene, the Librarian would spend her final days gathering the last specimens of humanity in order to replace those her husband had composed, relocating them to the lesser Ark where they would be safe from the Flood.

FALL OF THE ARK

The Master Builder prepared to make a final stand against the parasite at the greater Ark, where the last major remnant of Forerunner civilization dwelt. Mendicant Bias, now reunited with the Primordial in the form of the Gravemind, had led the Flood to the Ark's doorstep. To answer this threat, the Master Builder deployed a new ancilla—Offensive Bias—to direct what remained of the Forerunners' great fleets as well as Omega Halo. Here he set up a last line of defense against the Flood.

Yet this battle would not end in victory. With unimaginable numbers and power, the Flood devastated Omega Halo and the greater Ark, destroying all those who had taken shelter there. The last bastion for the Forerunners was now headed for the lesser Ark, where Bornstellar initiated plans to finally activate the Halo Array.

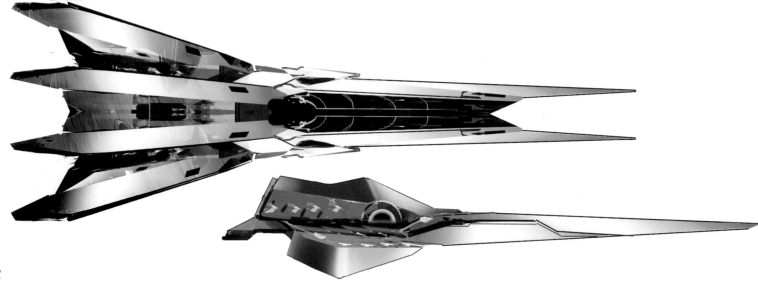

ACTIVATION OF THE ARRAY

After arriving at the lesser Ark, Bornstellar worked to distribute the seven ringworlds making up the final Halo Array around the galaxy. Each would be sent with its monitor; Bornstellar sent Chakas, now 343 Guilty Spark, to Alpha Halo, the first ring installation that he planned to activate. Not long after the ringworlds reached their correct positions, relays indicated that the Flood's vast fleets were now approaching the lesser Ark, led by Mendicant Bias.

Having narrowly survived the destruction of the greater Ark, Offensive Bias and what remained of his Forerunner fleet moved to meet the Flood at the edge of the galaxy, hoping to buy Bornstellar more time. During the battle, Bornstellar activated the Array, and Halo's destructive energies surged across the galaxy, annihilating both fleets, Forerunner and Flood. Mendicant Bias' manned vessels suddenly became lifeless, floating hulks—the ancilla's greatest strength, the Flood's immense numbers, had come to nothing. After neutralizing the last of the enemy ships, Offensive Bias apprehended its predecessor, and Bornstellar sentenced Mendicant Bias to permanent confinement on the lesser Ark.

REPOPULATION

In one fateful moment, the firing of Halo, the galaxy was rid of the Flood—at least for a time. In the decades that followed, the few Forerunners who had survived began to send specimens saved during the Conservation Measure back to their respective homeworlds, reseeding those places where they could now live free from the threat of the Flood. Some even hoped that the Librarian's efforts would allow humanity to rise to prominence once more, and become inheritors of all that the Forerunners had left behind, including the Mantle. They would be given the status of Reclaimers.

As time passed, the surviving Forerunners were lost from history, slipping into distant memory and legend. Those species that had been saved by the Librarian's efforts would later begin to pursue science and technology on their own. The Halo rings remained hidden and dormant, their monitors carefully safeguarding the immense installations and the dormant Flood specimens they held for research into a possible cure.

REMORSE

Long after the Forerunners, a fragment of Mendicant Bias managed to escape confinement and found his way into a local keyship—a vessel used to repopulate humans on Erde-Tyrene. Burrowing himself into the ship, Mendicant Bias departed from the Ark and headed toward the Milky Way. This time, however, the ancilla was not driven by wrath or madness, but rather remorse, attempting to make amends for his crimes against the Forerunners and the Mantle. His plan was to help humanity achieve the status of Reclaimers.

Unable to fully control the vessel in his weakened state, Mendicant was forced to alter course to seek additional aid from humanity's ancient allies—the San'Shyuum. Unfortunately, his efforts were cut short when the keyship crashed on Janjur Qom. Though Mendicant Bias had set out to fulfill the Librarian's designs for humankind, it would ironically lead to the formation of the Covenant, one of the greatest threats humanity would ever face.

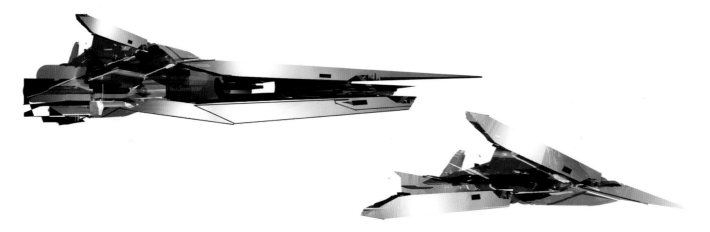

FORERUNNER FLEET

The final years of the war with the Flood proved harrowing for the Forerunners. The parasite spread across the galaxy with incredible speed. The Forerunners countered with their immense navy: vast fleets of warships, dreadnoughts, and fighters, battling the Flood over countless worlds. Such an exertion of raw military power has never since been recorded in the galaxy.

Initiated from a citadel on the lesser Ark far outside the galaxy, the activation of Halo proved both the value and the horror of the Master Builder's weapons. Although the Flood had been brought to an end for a time, responsibility for the Array now passed from Bornstellar and the Forerunners to the installations' individual monitors, such as Alpha Halo's 343 Guilty Spark. They alone carried the burden of safeguarding the rings across the long expanses of time that would follow.

Chase Toole

THE DREADNOUGHT

Many millennia after the Array's activation, the crashed Forerunner keyship—eventually known as the dreadnought—became an object of worship for the San'Shyuum on Janjur Qom. Their reverence for the ancient machine would split the San'Shyuum people, as they differed greatly on how it should be worshipped—a tension that would eventually ignite into full-scale war. This violence would lead to the creation of the Covenant, carrying destruction into the centuries to come.

Darren Bacon

Nearly one hundred thousand years after the activation of Halo, the San'Shyuum species, reseeded by the Librarian's Conservation Measure, began to explore the many Forerunner relics that remained on their planet.

THE GREAT JOURNEY

Ignorant of the events which had unfolded in their ancient past, the San'Shyuum developed their own religious beliefs around these awe-inspiring artifacts. Their core convictions revolved around the notion that the Forerunners had purposefully left these artifacts behind to guide those that came after them to divine transcendence—something they referred to as the Great Journey.

The most remarkable of these precious artifacts was a Forerunner keyship—the dreadnought—partially submerged in the Great Apothtea, an immense sea in Janjur Qom's northern hemisphere. Many San'Shyuum believed that they should access its inner systems for exploration, but this idea was met with fierce opposition.

The most devout of their kind believed that tampering with such artifacts was an act of heresy. Controversy erupted and a split quickly formed between the two major ideologies: the Stoics, who believed that artifacts should only be worshipped at a distance, and the less numerous Reformists, who argued that the artifacts were gifts to be explored, activated, and even dismantled if practical benefit could come from it.

CIVIL WAR

In 2200 BCE, this tension devolved into a violent civil conflict the San'Shyuum would refer to as the War of Wills: a bloody, century-long feud that culminated in a thousand heavily armed Reformists secretly infiltrating the dreadnought and barricading themselves inside. After forty days inside, the Reformists managed to activate the vessel's systems, and succeeded in igniting its ancient engines. Rising up from the sea and into Janjur Qom's sky, the Reformists had finally escaped their planet, leaving those who remained behind in sorrowful bewilderment.

For hundreds of years, these San'Shyuum would use the dreadnought to move from one system to another, finding numerous reliquary sites replete with artifacts and technologies left behind by their gods. Their philosophy grew around the Great Journey and vague prophecies of the Sacred Rings, generating the framework for a profound religious system—one which would drive all of their efforts in the future.

For a time, their progress would continue unimpeded, until they came in contact with a powerful warrior species that would not simply hand over the relics they sought— the start of a conflict even greater than the first.

JANJUR QOM
The San'Shyuum homeworld Janjur Qom, a water-rich planet with many dense jungles. The vast circular sea —the Great Apothtea—visible here was created when the dreadnought crashed long ago.

WAR OF BEGINNINGS

In 938 BCE, the San'Shyuum came upon Ulgethon, a rocky world that initially appeared to be uninhabited. The first pioneer detachment set their sights on an enormous mountain range that the dreadnought's luminary—a Forerunner machine that could track ancient artifacts—had targeted as a repository of hidden relics. They discovered that the mountains were inhabited by a saurian species known as the Sangheili.

THE SANGHEILI

Their first encounter seemed positive, though tense, but as soon as the Sangheili discovered the San'Shyuum's true intentions for the artifacts on their world, a bitter, devastating war broke out that would bring both species to their very knees.

Both the San'Shyuum and Sangheili had evolved on worlds rich with Forerunner artifacts, and both regarded them as holy, developing deeply religious beliefs about the architects of these machines. The Sangheili culture had a rigid, feudal structure with a heavy disposition toward combat, and became more focused on discovery and protection of Forerunner artifacts with each passing generation.

SACRED ARTIFACTS

Much like the San'Shyuum Stoics, they believed that the physical manipulation of such technology was sacrilegious to the highest degree, and punishable by death. When the Sangheili learned that the San'Shyuum intended to excavate and retrieve the sacred artifacts for themselves—as they evidently had with their dreadnought—they turned against the invaders.

The conflict over Ulgethon lasted a full year. By the end there was little left of the world but a charred husk filled with dead warriors and shattered ships. The Desecration of Ulgethon was only the start of the War of Beginnings, a conflict between these two species that would last decades.

As time passed, the Sangheili realized that they lacked enough firepower to halt the dreadnought's violent incursions. When they finally agreed to use Forerunner technology to defend their worlds, their now-augmented defenses sent the war into stalemate. In 852 BCE, a tentative truce was brokered between a Sangheili leader named Pelahsar the Strident and the San'Shyuum known as Breaking Shadow. The two leaders forgave the past crimes of their species and began working toward a peaceful alliance.

BIRTH OF THE COVENANT

This was eventually established by the Writ of Union, an agreement founded on the belief that despite their blood-soaked history, both species could work toward the same goal. The Covenant was born.

The focal point of the Covenant was the legend of Halo, the Sacred Rings which they believed held the ability to translate their physical bodies into divinity, just as it had with the Forerunners. This tragically mistaken interpretation governed all future actions of the Covenant, including their vicious genocidal war against humankind in the centuries that followed.

SAN'SHYUUM
The San'Shyuum matched Sangheili martial zeal with brilliant strategies and their dreadnought's irresistible firepower.

SANGHEILI
Saurian bipeds of impressive size and strength, the Sangheili evolved on the coastlines of their native cradle world, Sanghelios.

The Desecration of Ulgethon, and the War of Beginnings that raged in the decades that followed, proved to the San'Shyuum that—despite their powerful Forerunner dreadnought—they would be wise to forge an alliance with a species as strong and relentless as the Sangheili. During their first battle, the Sangheili courageously faced off against the ominous Forerunner dreadnought from warrens and ridges across the face of Ulgethon, using the most formidable weapons of war they could then fashion. In the years following the war, all Sangheili weapons and ships would be upgraded with Forerunner technology, and ornately styled by the San'Shyuum to befit the newly-founded Covenant.

David Heidhoff

FORMATION OF THE COVENANT

The Writ of Union between the two founding species of the Covenant was not a simple coalition, but rather a contract of requirements and responsibilities for both the San'Shyuum and the Sangheili. In addition to both species laying down their arms, they commissioned the construction of a shared homeworld: the Holy City of High Charity. From this massive fortress, the Covenant subdued and integrated new species into their alliance; together, they moved ever forward in their quest for Forerunner technology, and, ultimately, the activation of the Sacred Rings.

David Heidhoff

THE BARGAIN

As part of the Writ, the San'Shyuum agreed to forsake their dreadnought, decommissioning it permanently. It would eventually be used as the primary source of power for the Covenant Holy City of High Charity, a mobile homeworld for the alliance. The San'Shyuum would also adopt the Sangheili language as their own in response to the sheer number of Sangheili in the Covenant. This was viewed by the Sangheili as the greatest single concession the San'Shyuum made, effectively establishing their own culture as the primary foundation for the Covenant.

To the San'Shyuum, this was a non-issue, as they had few surviving cultural practices of interest; they could easily trade their language for power. They established a triumvirate of ruling 'Hierarchs' at the head of the Covenant. This formalized the convention that the San'Shyuum, commonly referred to as Prophets, were responsible for government, religion, and science, whereas the Sangheili, known as Elites, would retain the role of military protection, exploration, and the recovery of Forerunner artifacts.

Thus began a long relationship born of skepticism and distrust, but now unified under the mutual belief in the Great Journey, and the godhood promised by the Sacred Rings.

HIGH CHARITY

After the dreadnought had been decommissioned, it was nestled in the slowly constructed shell of High Charity—itself built on materials recovered from the San'Shyuum homeworld. As well as providing seemingly unlimited power and energy, the dreadnought's relic-detecting luminary was duplicated and equipped on a number of key Sangheili ships, leading their fleets throughout space to one Forerunner site after another.

COVENANT SPECIES

GRUNT
Species: Unggoy
(*Monachus frigus*)
Homeworld: Balaho

Squat and diminutive, often deployed as expendable cannon fodder.

DRONE
Species: Yanme'e
(*Turpis rex*)
Homeworld: Palamok

Capable of limited flight and utilized in large numbers to overwhelm and distract enemy forces.

SKIRMISHER
Species: Kig-Yar
(*Perosus latrunculus*)
Homeworld: Eayn

Distinctive due to their plumage, remarkably swift and agile in combat.

JACKAL
Species: Kig-Yar
(*Perosus latrunculus*)
Homeworld: Eayn

Varying in look across the species, energy shielding offers protection to combat squads.

THE COVENANT EXPANDS

Another Forerunner technology employed by the Covenant was the Engineers, or Huragok as they were originally called by their creators. These were machines made to look like living creatures—a composite of nano-mechanical surrogate organs. The Huragok helped to repair and preserve Covenant machines, and also to dismantle and reverse-engineer any discovered Forerunner devices.

Over the centuries, the Covenant encountered many species and conscripted them into their hegemony, offering the promise of the Great Journey to all who served and believed. At the height of their empire, the Covenant included species such as the Lekgolo, commonly known as Hunters; the Yanme'e, which were called Drones; the Kig-Yar, comprised of Jackals and Skirmishers; the Unggoy, generally referred to as Grunts; and the Jiralhanae, or Brutes. In addition, a number of fringe species that were too small or scattered in numbers to justify full membership were still employed to various ends within the empire.

There was one species, however, whose chance discovery in the 26th century would come as a great surprise to the San'Shyuum. This species represented the most significant challenge to the Covenant's formerly unquestioned dominance: humanity.

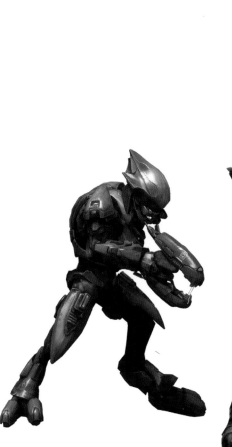

ELITE
Species: Sangheili
(*Macto cognatus*)
Homeworld: Sanghelios

Proud and noble warriors, serving across a wide spectrum of lethal classes and roles.

BRUTE
Species: Jiralhanae
(*Servus ferox*)
Homeworld: Doisac

Relatively primitive, their incredible strength and ferocity is used in shock trooper roles.

HUNTER
Species: Mgalekgolo
(*Ophis congregatio*)
Homeworld: Te

Operate in pairs, representing a single colony of Lekgolo. Extraordinarily powerful and unyielding.

RISE OF HUMANITY

One hundred thousand years would pass before humanity returned to the stars. During the long ages that followed Halo's activation, the inhabitants of Earth, confined to their cradle world, lost all knowledge of the Forerunners and of their own forebears' ancient history.

Only in the 20th century would humans escape Earth's atmosphere and once again ascend into the inky depths of space. First, in the lower reaches of Earth's orbit, then to other worlds in the Sol system, and eventually turning their thoughts to stars that were once out of reach.

By 2080, Earth's nations had put together joint efforts to colonize Luna, Mars, and a handful of other sites in the Sol system. Despite the daunting technological challenge of embedding sustainable populations on these worlds, new scientific innovations eventually made it a reality, and the interplanetary colonies saw growth and prosperity during these early years.

In the mid-22nd century, two militant movements emerged among Earth's colonies, dramatically altering the political landscape. The first, originating in Mars' mining city of Oenotria, was known as the Koslovics, after Vladimir Koslov and his family. They were miners turned activists, railing against what they saw as financial exploitation by the corporations that dominated the colony.

After the violent takeover of three major mining facilities, the Koslovics were deemed terrorists by the United Nations. Their ideas, however, gained momentum across Mars and rural parts of Luna, among people who felt government-sponsored companies were violating the rights of colonists.

The other hostile ideology, the Frieden movement, grew out of Katreus, a major city on the Jovian moon Europa. Although the term 'Frieden' is German for 'peace,' the movement quickly escalated to violence. In 2158, the Friedens targeted an embassy in the Europan city of Thynia, leveling the structure with military-grade explosives. As with the Koslovics, the United Nations labeled the Friedens terrorists, and dispatched UN Colonial Advisors to the Jovian moon of Io to help organize policing efforts.

In the years that followed, few colonists remained neutral, and both militant groups grew rapidly in support and resources. The United Nations lacked the military capability to prevent this, and the Koslovics and Friedens spread their influence and activities largely unchecked across Mars, Luna, and the Jovian Moons.

Eventually the two sides clashed, due to their directly opposing politics. By 2160, the terrorist campaigns had escalated to full-scale war, as the factions fought the Jovian Moon Campaigns—foreshadowing the devastating Interplanetary War.

THE INTERPLANETARY WAR

The brutal and harrowing Interplanetary War, waged primarily between the Koslovics and the Friedens, spanned much of the Sol system. The war would forever change the way Earth and her colonies were governed. Of particular significance was the formation of the United Nations Space Command, a powerful, unified military force designed to subdue colonial hostilities.

Jean-Sébastien Rossbach

The death toll of the Jovian Moons campaigns was substantial, but by late 2161, the battle between the Koslovics and the Friedens had subsided; the bloodshed ceased for several months, and some speculated that the worst had passed. In February 2162, however, a series of bombings in South America began a nineteen-month conflict that would come to be known as the Rainforest Wars. Engagements spread across the entire continent, reigniting violence throughout the Sol system.

BATTLE ON MARS

In November of 2163, the Friedens suffered a critical loss, as their leader, Nadja Mielke, was assassinated on her way to a command center in the Europa city called Pelagon. This enraged the Friedens, and in December they retaliated with nearly all the military assets at their disposal. A large-scale campaign against Argyre Planitia, the hub of Koslovic activity on Mars, obliterated the city within hours. More fighting occurred during the weeks that followed, as the Koslovic forces scattered into the city's outskirts.

The United Nations had by now formed a composite military force—which would eventually be called the United Nations Space Command (UNSC)—and deployed it to the Martian territories' most combat-intensive area. By January 2164, the conflict historically known as the Interplanetary War had officially begun. The battle on Mars lasted two full years as the United Nations bombed Koslovic remnants, stamping out any Martian opposition. Despite the vast death toll, there was little concern on Earth about the ethics of these strikes;

THE SOL SYSTEM

PLUTO
Slipspace monitoring station

OORT CLOUD
ONI shipyards

EUROPA
Xenobiology labs

GANYMEDE
Research habitats

CALLISTO
UNSC naval depot

IO
UNSC listening post

LUNA
Naval academy, canopy
settlements

JUPITER
Gas mining, industrial
habitats

VENUS
Failed terraforming project

EARTH
Homeworld of the human race

most felt that they were justified as a way to prevent the violence from spreading to their own soil.

Although the Koslovics suffered extensive losses in the early parts of the Martian assault, they continued to thrive on Luna and in isolated parts of Earth. In August 2167, however, Vladimir Koslov and his family were killed in a bombing near Lake Autolycus on Luna. While the UNSC denied involvement, many believed that the Friedens were not capable of carrying out such an attack. Whatever the cause, this act severed the head of the Koslovic movement.

CEASEFIRE
Despite some difficulty on the UNSC's part, Europa, Io, Ganymede, and Callisto all saw large-scale invasions by

Marine forces, resulting in the destruction of hundreds of Frieden bases and weapon caches. The last of the Friedens fought savagely under Oscar Bauer, nephew of Nadja Mielke, but by mid-2169, little remained of their movement.

Before long, the last vestiges of both the Koslovics and the Friedens were apprehended by the UNSC. The United Nations penned the Callisto Treaty, a ceasefire agreement that gave the UNSC complete military jurisdiction in all colonial territories. The treaty was signed in March 2170 on the Jovian moon of Callisto. With it, a single authority came into existence, called the Unified Earth Government (UEG). This would be the seat of power and governance for all of Earth's colonies in the future.

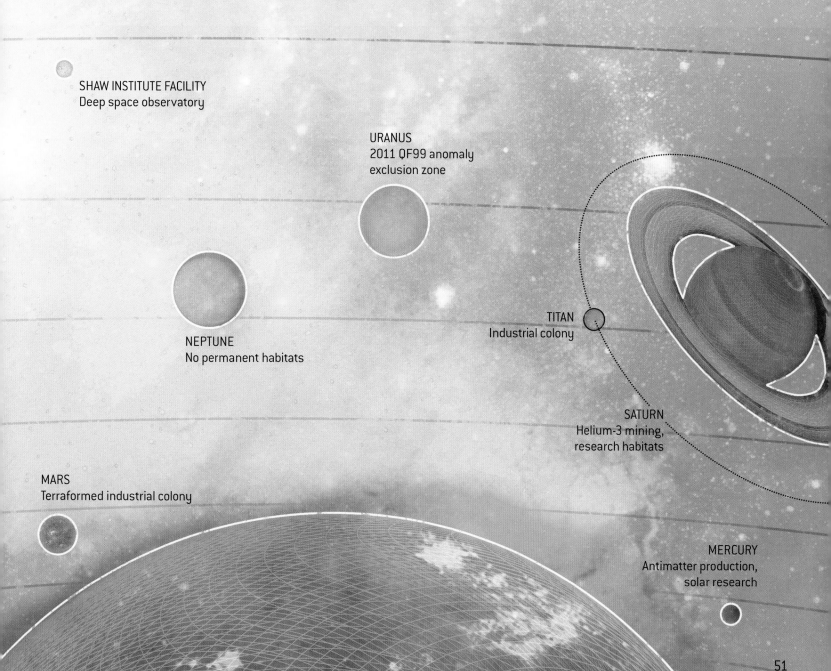

SHAW INSTITUTE FACILITY
Deep space observatory

URANUS
2011 QF99 anomaly
exclusion zone

NEPTUNE
No permanent habitats

TITAN
Industrial colony

SATURN
Helium-3 mining,
research habitats

MARS
Terraformed industrial colony

MERCURY
Antimatter production,
solar research

DOMUS DIASPORA

Often referred to as 'The Colonial Era,' the *Domus Diaspora* is remembered as the greatest colonization effort of humans in history. With the development of faster-than-light travel through what was known as slipstream space, humanity gained access to distant worlds. Leaving the Sol system to voyage into the deep, they inhabited remote star systems scattered across the Orion Arm of the Milky Way galaxy.

Jean-Sébastien Rossbach

COLONY SUPPORT SHIP
Deployed from vessels like the Odyssey, *support craft carried the first wave of colonial occupation. Pioneers used these ships as groundside hubs, dispatching research and supply convoys between the burgeoning new communities.*

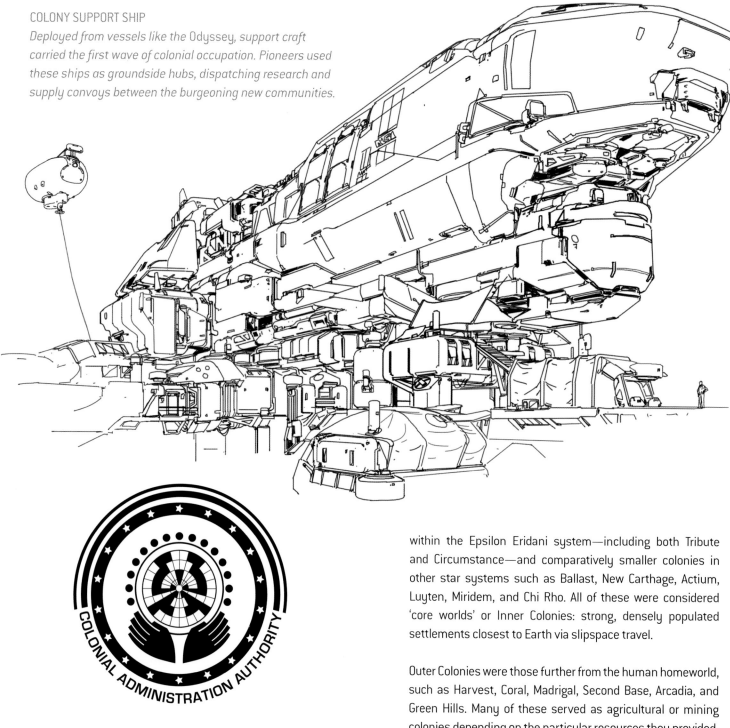

COLONIAL ADMINISTRATION AUTHORITY

THE COLONIES

In 2362, centuries after the Interplanetary War, the very first extrasolar colonization vessel—the *Odyssey*—launched from its mooring platform in orbit over Luna, alongside nearly one hundred other colony ships. In the weeks that followed, these vessels arrived at their destinations and began the elaborate and protracted process of terraforming alien worlds. This vast exodus was organized by the UEG's Colonial Administration Authority, after many long years of preparation.

The first extrasolar planet reached by humans was Epsilon Eridani II, aptly named 'Reach' by its first inhabitants. In the decades to come, it would become humanity's colonial center of military power. A number of other colonies were established

within the Epsilon Eridani system—including both Tribute and Circumstance—and comparatively smaller colonies in other star systems such as Ballast, New Carthage, Actium, Luyten, Miridem, and Chi Rho. All of these were considered 'core worlds' or Inner Colonies: strong, densely populated settlements closest to Earth via slipspace travel.

Outer Colonies were those further from the human homeworld, such as Harvest, Coral, Madrigal, Second Base, Arcadia, and Green Hills. Many of these served as agricultural or mining colonies depending on the particular resources they provided.

By the 26th century, over 800 individual colonies were spread across the Orion Arm, including planets, moons, asteroids, mining facilities, and relay stations. Humankind saw unprecedented growth and development during this time; yet despite this progress, hostilities broke out in some of the more remote settlements. A number of civilian uprisings against Earth's control occurred from 2475 to 2483.

The response from the Colonial Military Administration (CMA) was swift and severe, but its heavy-handed tactics backfired, hardening resistance. Even stronger and more aggressive dissidents took the political stage, beginning what would be the longest period of civil unrest humanity had ever seen.

THE INSURRECTION

In 2487, the newly-established People's Occupation and the Secessionist Union submitted formal requests on behalf of a dozen worlds, demanding independence from Earth. With tensions rising on both sides, violence once again rocked the Outer Colonies.

THE CALLISTO INCIDENT

It was the *Callisto* Incident that tipped the scales. In January 2494 the patrolling UNSC *Callisto* performed a routine inspection of a colonial vessel. It went tragically awry: shots were fired, and thirty colonists were killed. The entire region was spun into an uproar.

Shortly afterwards, the *Callisto* was hijacked by local terrorists, who killed the crew and used the ship against UNSC forces. The UNSC responded aggressively: having subdued and recaptured the ship, they cracked down across the territory, sparking rebellion throughout the Outer Colonies.

COLONEL WATTS

The Insurrection began. Guerrilla cells in the Secessionist Union assaulted colonial embassies and government buildings, and, in June 2494, rebels under the leadership of Ex-UNSC Marine Colonel Robert Watts orchestrated a series of military operations against the Outer Colony world Eridanus II. Before the CMA could respond, the local authorities had already been overrun by the Secessionist Union; and by January 2495, Eridanus II had been claimed by the rebels.

This led to the UNSC's first full-scale response to the Insurrection, Operation: CHARLEMAGNE, a campaign to retake Eridanus II. The UNSC successfully recaptured the colony and drove Watts and his forces into hiding.

OPERATION: KALEIDOSCOPE

Victory, however, remained out of reach. Rebel forces continued their guerrilla campaign, inflicting massive losses. By the start of the 26th century, the UNSC changed tactics, initiating Operation: KALEIDOSCOPE, a series of highly-classified surgical strikes against prominent rebel leaders. Over the next five years, UNSC assassins targeted key rebel commanders, killing key figures such as Molin Saal, Jerald Ander, Standish Kable, and Elanor Kef. By 2509, however, many rebel cells had combined under the leadership of Robert Watts, proudly referring to themselves as the United Rebel Front.

The UNSC and the Front continued to trade blows. A Watts-led invasion force retook Eridanus II in January of 2513. Months later, a UNSC battlegroup assaulted the planet in what would be the first part of Operation: TREBUCHET, a final, brutal UNSC crackdown on all rebel activity. Although the loss of life was extraordinary, the UNSC won several notable victories, including the recapture of Eridanus II.

Despite this, the turmoil and chaos of the Insurrection continued unabated. It was becoming increasingly clear that conventional military means would not end this war.

COLONEL WATTS

Once an esteemed and decorated member of the UNSC Marine Corps, Robert Watts defected after years of blood-soaked fighting on the front lines of the colonial conflict. This event served to escalate the Insurrection, as Watts led rebel forces from Eridanus II and eventually went on to spearhead the violent coalition of insurgents known as the United Rebel Front.

The Insurrection left millions dead. Remarkably, the civil war had been predicted as early as 2491, by Doctor Elias Carver. His study into the political and security situation of Earth and its colonies, known as the 'Carver Findings,' pointed to the imminent breakdown of government in human space. Though Carver's report did not prevent the Insurrection, it proved influential on some—notably, Doctor Catherine Halsey.

Jean-Sébastien Rossbach

SPARTANS

With no end to the Insurrection in sight, extreme measures were now being pursued. The most significant of these was the creation of the Spartans. Building on earlier successes, Doctor Halsey initiated the SPARTAN-II project: full-scale production of biologically-augmented, armor-enhanced super-soldiers. These Spartans became living legends, revolutionizing the art of war. Although they would play a major role in quelling the rebellion, a common threat would soon galvanize humanity and send the Spartans headlong into a conflict that would bring humanity to the brink of extinction.

Jean-Sébastien Rossbach

The Insurrection proved that humanity's survival could not be secured by traditional military methods. Even before the rebellion, the UNSC's Office of Naval Intelligence (ONI) had secretly launched the ORION project, intending to engineer super-soldiers: a precision combat force capable of stemming the tide of unrest swiftly and silently. But in 2506, for cost and performance reasons, ONI decided to abort ORION and reintegrate its personnel into the existing UNSC forces.

SPARTAN

By 2508, with the Insurrection raging, ONI once again saw the need to revisit this unconventional strategy. They recruited Doctor Catherine Halsey, a young but brilliant scientist who would not balk at taking whatever steps necessary to achieve ONI's goals. Halsey set into motion two parallel projects: SPARTAN-II and MJOLNIR, both of equal significance to her designs.

Halsey believed that effective super-soldiers needed to be cultivated at a young age. In September 2517, she initiated the first stage of her plan. Halsey selected children who had impressive strength, speed, and intellect—the most advanced six-year-olds across human space.

The children were abducted and brought secretly to a highly classified training facility on the colony of Reach. To hide this crime, ONI replaced the children with rapidly-grown 'flash-clones.' This highly illegal procedure created convincing but short-lived replicas of the abductees; the clones all died soon after. On Reach, the abducted children were aggressively trained for several years by the renowned drill instructor Chief Petty Officer Franklin Mendez, learning a vast number of combat skills and tactics.

In March 2525, SPARTAN-II entered its second phase: the physical augmentation of each child, forcing their bodies to receive a range of surgical and biochemical enhancements. The process was extremely traumatic, leaving many crippled or dead. Despite the loss of nearly half the candidates, the results were positive: the young Spartans were nothing short of extraordinary. Even at fourteen years old, they were stronger, more resilient, and faster than any human before. This was proven in a raid on a rebel base hidden within the asteroid field near Eridanus II, in which the Spartans managed to finally capture the elusive rebel leader Colonel Robert Watts.

MJOLNIR

The last phase was the integration of Project: MJOLNIR, the most advanced combat armor system ever created by humans. Mjolnir Mark IV armor was developed on the distant world of Chi Ceti IV and entered the final stages of production in November 2525. The melding of biologically enhanced super-soldiers with state-of-the-art armor marked the completion of the SPARTAN-II program, resulting in the most remarkable soldiers the species had ever produced.

Almost immediately both man and machine were tested, as the Spartans were called to defend Chi Ceti IV from a newfound enemy. The creation of the Spartans came at the most critical hour in human history; although they had been devised to end the Insurrection, this handful of warriors would be humanity's best defense against a far more menacing foe—the Covenant.

DOCTOR CATHERINE HALSEY

The remarkably brilliant intellect of Catherine Elizabeth Halsey was evident early in her life. She had completed two doctoral thesis papers by the age of fifteen, and became a scientific advisor of ONI in 2515, spearheading SPARTAN-II and MJOLNIR only two years later. Although her methods and ethics would later be questioned, these two projects played a substantial role in humanity's survival in the decades that followed.

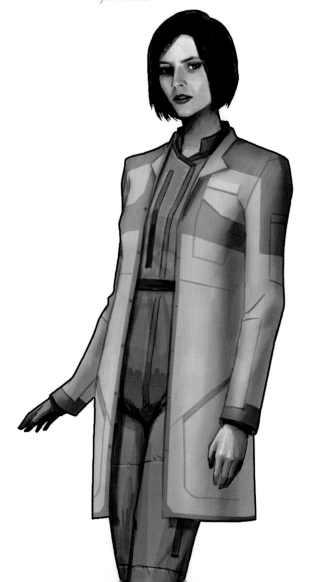

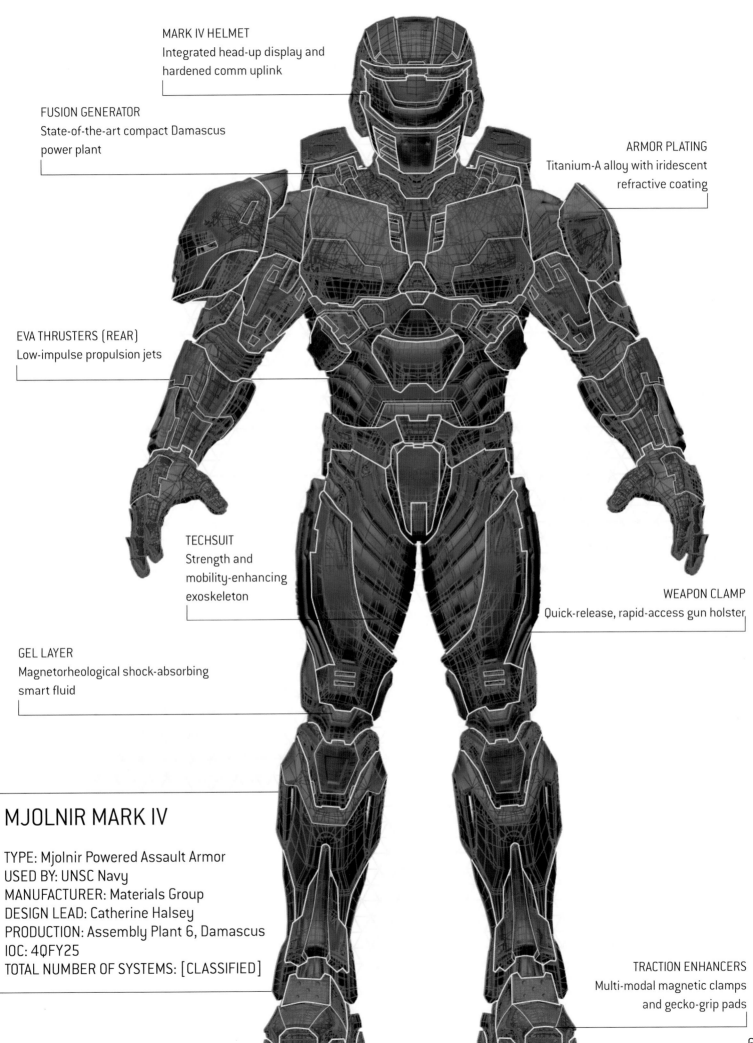

MARK IV HELMET
Integrated head-up display and
hardened comm uplink

FUSION GENERATOR
State-of-the-art compact Damascus
power plant

ARMOR PLATING
Titanium-A alloy with iridescent
refractive coating

EVA THRUSTERS (REAR)
Low-impulse propulsion jets

TECHSUIT
Strength and
mobility-enhancing
exoskeleton

WEAPON CLAMP
Quick-release, rapid-access gun holster

GEL LAYER
Magnetorheological shock-absorbing
smart fluid

MJOLNIR MARK IV

TYPE: Mjolnir Powered Assault Armor
USED BY: UNSC Navy
MANUFACTURER: Materials Group
DESIGN LEAD: Catherine Halsey
PRODUCTION: Assembly Plant 6, Damascus
IOC: 4QFY25
TOTAL NUMBER OF SYSTEMS: [CLASSIFIED]

TRACTION ENHANCERS
Multi-modal magnetic clamps
and gecko-grip pads

FIRST CONTACT AT HARVEST

It was only by extraordinary chance that a patrolling Covenant vessel stumbled across a human trade route adjacent to the Epsilon Indi star system. Despite their colonial expansion, humanity had remained secluded in their sliver of the Orion Arm, while the Covenant war machine marauded across space, seizing any relics of the Forerunners they could find. The remote agricultural world of Harvest would become the site not only of first contact, but also of the opening salvos of the traumatic three-decades-long conflict known as the Covenant War.

Jean-Sébastien Rossbach

The Covenant had been drawn to Harvest by one of their luminaries, which had targeted what the aliens believed to be an extraordinary cache of relics on the surface. The alliance was established with the purpose of searching out Forerunner artifacts, and it appeared that Harvest was full of these sacred and mysterious treasures. However, the truth was very different.

THE ORACLE

Locked aboard the Forerunner dreadnought which powered the city of High Charity, the ancilla once known as Mendicant Bias was now referred to as the Oracle. Though only intermittently active, he was periodically consulted by the San'Shyuum Prophets to aid their decisions. The Oracle revealed to three curious Prophets that humanity had been designated 'Reclaimers': the species selected by the Forerunners as inheritors of their legacy. It was not, then, a cache of relics that had attracted the luminary—it was the humans themselves. The three San'Shyuum concealed this shattering revelation and the secret became a tool in their own struggle for power.

FIRST CONTACT

Meanwhile a single Covenant ship was sent to make peaceful first contact with the humans on the planet's surface—a mission that went terribly wrong. The tense ceremony was interrupted by mistaken weapons fire from a lone Covenant soldier, igniting a bloody gunfight between Harvest's raw and edgy local militia and the Jiralhanae—the Covenant's brutish, shock-trooper species. A brief but ferocious siege of the planet by the Covenant cruiser *Rapid Conversion* followed. Though its Jiralhanae commander, the chieftain Maccabeus, perished during the battle, the Covenant seized control of the entire colony.

FALSE PROPHETS

The San'Shyuum Prophets who had discovered the truth about humanity exploited this information, becoming the High Prophet triumvirate controlling all Covenant matters. Rather than offer the humans a truce or an opportunity to join their alliance, the Prophets painted them as vermin, infesting and desecrating the Forerunners' holy possessions. Ord Casto, Lod Mron, and Hod Rumnt, now known respectively as the Prophets of Truth, Regret, and Mercy, would maintain their power throughout the remainder of the Covenant War—a war to exterminate the human species.

Unaware of the devastating assault on Harvest, the UNSC first discovered that something was amiss when communication was lost with the colony. They dispatched the scout ship *Argo* to investigate in April 2525—but the vessel was destroyed almost immediately upon entering the system. Fearing rebel occupation of the colony, and blind to the true nature of the enemy, a battle group was deployed.

THE TERROR BEGINS

The battle group discovered a single Covenant warship orbiting Harvest, and found that the colony had been bombarded from space and nearly obliterated. Two of the human ships were swiftly disabled by the Covenant vessel, while the lone *Heracles* desperately engaged its slipspace drive and narrowly escaped. The ship returned with a single, chilling message: an alliance of aliens calling themselves the Covenant were bent on the complete eradication of humankind.

The UNSC immediately went on high alert. Vice Admiral Preston Cole assembled the largest fleet yet deployed by the UNSC, and brought it to Harvest in March 2526. A total of forty

warships under Cole's command engaged the alien enemy. Though Cole was victorious, the UNSC still lost thirteen vessels to a single Covenant warship; a grim assessment of the strength of their newfound foe. Meanwhile, reports of other colonies losing contact began to multiply.

The world of Harvest had not seen the last of its struggles. Determined to take back this colony, and unaware of how vast their enemy truly was, the UNSC redoubled their efforts, battling Covenant ground forces across Harvest's mangled surface and in the space around it. This conflict continued for five years, until at last the Covenant released its hold and fled the Epsilon Indi system.

ANCIENT SECRETS

The UNSC eventually discovered the reason for the Covenant's persistence on Harvest. Hidden in the planet's uncharted arctic regions was an alien structure that predated the human colony, and even the Covenant itself: a buried Forerunner facility. Humanity started to piece together clues about the Covenant's military goals, and also began to open their eyes to the secrets of the Forerunners.

What the UNSC did not know at this time was that the technology of the Forerunners would ultimately present their greatest hope against the seemingly unstoppable Covenant—though this would become clear only at the very threshold of humanity's extinction.

The first few months of the Covenant War saw many swift and gruesome tragedies strike the Outer Colonies. Attacking fleets would first cripple a colony's ability to call for help, then unleash vicious orbital strikes on population centers, destroying any hope of mounting a resistance. Sometimes the battle would be taken to the colony's surface, with UNSC military forces engaging with the Covenant across the very worlds they had previously called home. This contest may have been futile given the Covenant's overwhelming technological superiority, but from it came stories of valor: for the first time in millennia, humanity was united against a single enemy.

Jean-Sébastien Rossbach

SHIELD WORLD

Toward the tail end of the five-year conflict at Harvest, the events involving the UNSC *Spirit of Fire* and her crew offered eerie clues to what the war would hold for humanity—and a solitary hope for victory, which would only become apparent decades later. The ship would find its way to one of the Forerunners' astonishing shield worlds, teeming with impossibly powerful technology—and hiding a dark secret.

Jean-Sébastien Rossbach

SPIRIT OF FIRE

On February 4, 2531, the UNSC *Spirit of Fire*, commanded by Captain James Cutter, began military operations on the besieged colony of Harvest. This immense support vessel deployed troops and materiel to the surface, overwhelming the Covenant's last remaining groundside forces while the war raged on in other parts of human space.

When the ship's crew discovered that the Covenant had been excavating an ancient alien facility that predated humanity's occupation of this world, they immediately sent a team to the site, including leading xenobiologist Professor Ellen Anders.

The team discovered a holographic map room pointing to the human colony of Arcadia. The Covenant, for reasons that remained a mystery, was already en route to the location; *Spirit of Fire* followed closely behind. Upon arrival, the *Spirit*'s Sergeant John Forge fought alongside Spartans originally deployed by the UNSC to defend the planet. Their efforts forced back the Covenant invasion, buying time to investigate the aliens' presence on this colony.

The Covenant had discovered something in Forerunner ruins deep in Arcadia's jungles, but before the *Spirit*'s crew could determine their target, their enemies abducted Professor Anders from the artifact site and fled into slipspace, with the *Spirit of Fire* in pursuit. The chase took them all the way to a remote, artificial world unlike anything humanity had ever seen: a shield world, one of the Forerunners' unbelievable creations built during their war with the Flood.

DESPERATION

On the surface of this strange new world, the *Spirit*'s crew encountered this ancient parasite. The Flood had somehow escaped its containment on the installation. After narrowly surviving the outbreak, Cutter dispatched forces to take Anders back. The Covenant's plan now became clear. The Forerunners had kept an entire fleet of powerful warships within this particular construct, ready to be deployed at the command of a 'Reclaimer'—a title that Anders now discovered had been bequeathed to humans by the ancients. When Anders was forced by the Covenant to activate this fleet, *Spirit*'s crew realized that they needed to destroy the shield world—taking the Covenant, the Flood, and the Forerunner fleet with it.

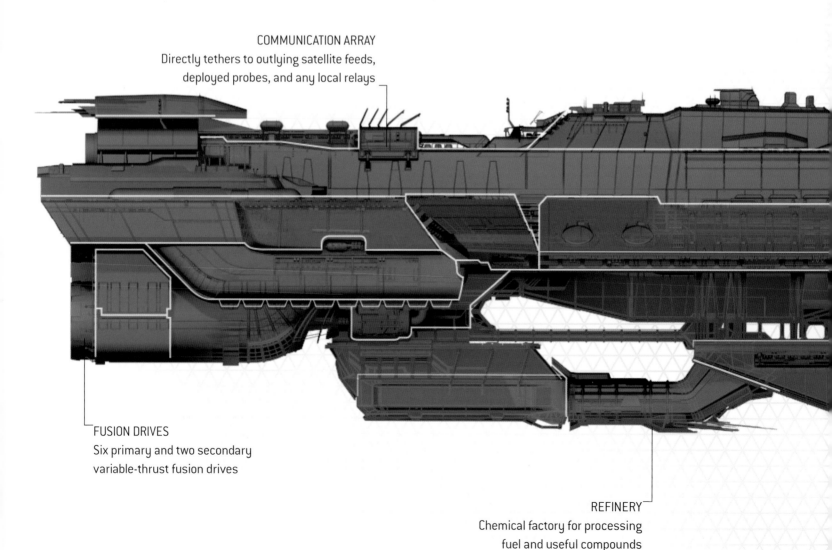

COMMUNICATION ARRAY
Directly tethers to outlying satellite feeds, deployed probes, and any local relays

FUSION DRIVES
Six primary and two secondary variable-thrust fusion drives

REFINERY
Chemical factory for processing fuel and useful compounds

In order to do this, the *Spirit* would have to relinquish her slipspace drive, converting it into a bomb. Sacrificing his own life, Sergeant Forge activated the drive, causing a stellar collapse of the artificial star at the world's center and completely obliterating it. *Spirit of Fire* narrowly escaped the destruction, but the ship was now stranded, forced to crawl at sublight speeds back to human-occupied space.

Although *Spirit of Fire* would be declared by the UNSC 'lost with all hands' on February 10, 2534, the remaining crew remained in cryostorage as the ship began the long journey back home. The story of the *Spirit of Fire* was not yet finished.

SPIRIT OF FIRE

CLASS: *Phoenix*-class Support Ship
LENGTH: 2,500 meters
PRIMARY ARMAMENT: 22B6R3 MAC Battery
KEEL LAID: 2470
LAUNCHED: 2473
CAPTAIN: Captain James Cutter
MOTTO: *Exitus Acta Probat*

PHOENIX
Drawn from the ship's rich history, the phoenix design on the Spirit of Fire*'s crew emblem represents humanity's ability to rise from the ashes of adversity.*

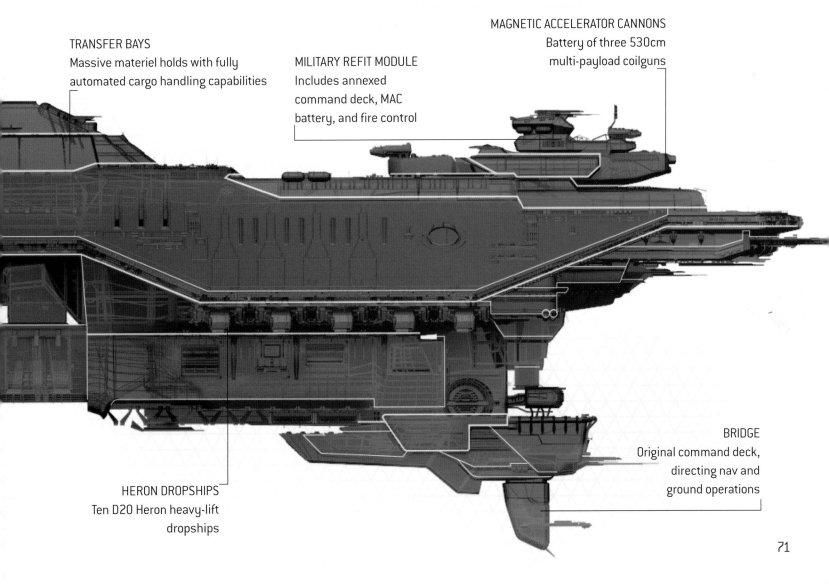

MAGNETIC ACCELERATOR CANNONS
Battery of three 530cm multi-payload coilguns

TRANSFER BAYS
Massive materiel holds with fully automated cargo handling capabilities

MILITARY REFIT MODULE
Includes annexed command deck, MAC battery, and fire control

BRIDGE
Original command deck, directing nav and ground operations

HERON DROPSHIPS
Ten D20 Heron heavy-lift dropships

TIDE OF DESTRUCTION

In the first few years of the war, the Covenant had already discovered over two dozen human colonies—and destroyed them without warning or mercy. Before the UNSC understood the severity of this new threat, entire worlds had blinked out of existence, using a procedure the Covenant referred to as 'cleansing.' The immense alien fleets would unleash superheated plasma across a planet to scour it clean of human life. Sections of the world's surface would be entirely melted, leaving a lifeless, vitrified substance—leading the humans to refer to this procedure as 'glassing.'

Jean-Sébastien Rossbach

MASSACRE

The Covenant dominated space combat. They possessed naval and weapon technology that greatly surpassed that of humankind. Spartans, however, offered a glimmer of hope for the UNSC. Humanity's super-soldiers were not only a match for the Covenant's formidable, Sangheili-led military on the ground, but also in space, as they could infiltrate and execute missions within enemy vessels—in rare cases, even taking down entire warships and fleets with only a handful of operatives.

Despite the victories Spartans had won against the Covenant, little overall could be done to stem the swelling tide of destruction. This period would come to be called the Massacre of the Outer Colonies, and would see the ruin of dozens of human worlds. By 2535, most of the Outer Colonies were charred husks, laid waste in short, brutal engagements. Evacuation craft that managed to escape were often hunted down and destroyed before fleeing the system; only on occasion would pockets of refugees survive to reach the relative safety of another colony.

A handful of human worlds managed to prepare defenses in advance, supported by the UNSC fleets and detachments of troops. But even in those scenarios, the Covenant rarely needed to take the fight to the ground, as their naval strength usually subdued the world without difficulty.

THE COLE PROTOCOL

The UNSC eventually recognized that the Covenant were often led to human worlds by data retrieved from colonies which they had already attacked. Navigation databases recovered from human vessels had also offered the Covenant slipspace routes to other colonies, drawing the enemy to new prey.

To prevent this, in the early years of the war Admiral Preston Cole submitted a universal standing order commonly referred to as the 'Cole Protocol.' This order dictated procedures for ships departing from any engagement with Covenant forces: navigation databases had to be destroyed, all on-board AIs had to be purged, and ships could only leave on random course headings. This was to ensure that the Covenant could not discover the location of Earth or any remaining Inner Colonies.

SHIPS OF WAR

These are just a handful of the naval vessels which played a role in the nearly thirty-year-long war. Despite the skill and audacity of many of their commanders, the UNSC's ships were physically outclassed by the Covenant's in size, speed, and firepower. This proved to humanity that it would take more than grit and guns to win this war.

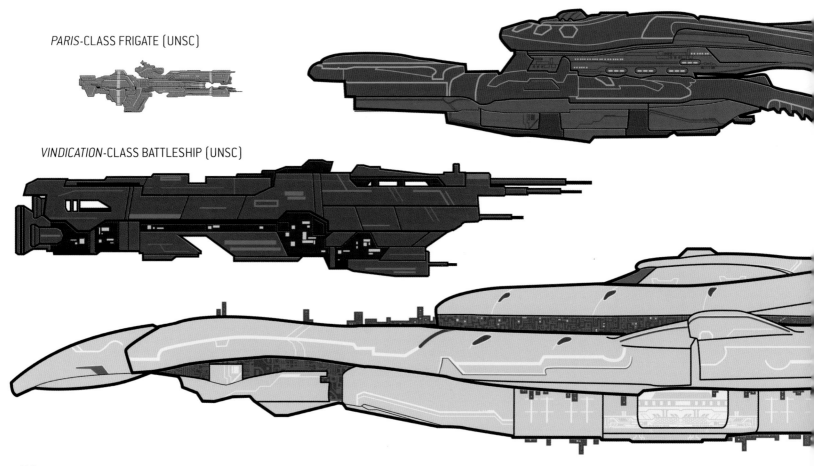

PARIS-CLASS FRIGATE (UNSC)

VINDICATION-CLASS BATTLESHIP (UNSC)

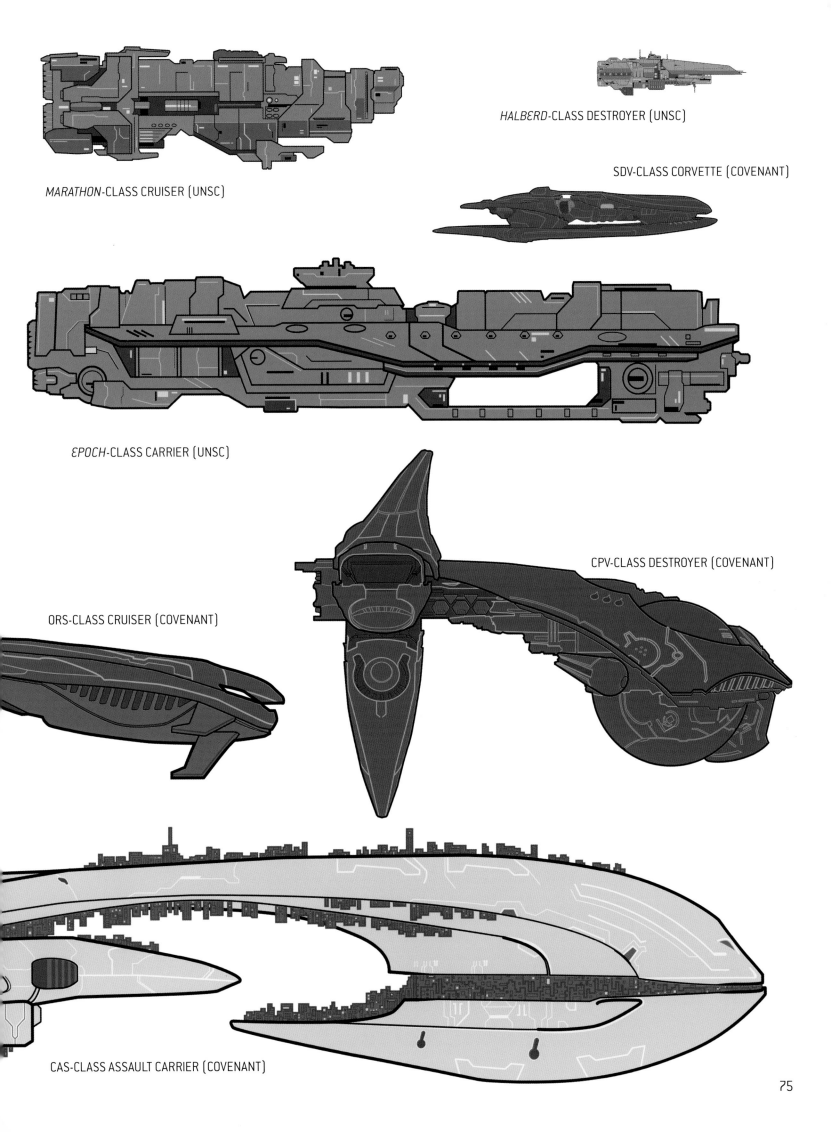

MARATHON-CLASS CRUISER (UNSC)

HALBERD-CLASS DESTROYER (UNSC)

SDV-CLASS CORVETTE (COVENANT)

EPOCH-CLASS CARRIER (UNSC)

CPV-CLASS DESTROYER (COVENANT)

ORS-CLASS CRUISER (COVENANT)

CAS-CLASS ASSAULT CARRIER (COVENANT)

SPARTAN-III PROGRAM

Despite its secrecy, the SPARTAN-II program had been such a success that it had attracted the attention of the ambitious and shrewd Colonel James Ackerson. Although he was a rival of Doctor Halsey's, Ackerson acknowledged her genius. Piggybacking on her advancements, he secretly proposed a successor to the program: SPARTAN-III. Ackerson wanted to streamline the previous hardware by providing a more affordable armor system than Mjolnir, and to build on technological improvements in the past few years to generate more candidates. For Ackerson, more Spartans meant more victories.

The highly-classified SPARTAN-III program began in December 2531, and was engineered on the secret world of Onyx. To run it, Ackerson recruited Chief Petty Officer Franklin Mendez, who trained the previous class of Spartans, and Kurt-051—now known as Lieutenant Commander Kurt Ambrose—a Spartan-II with impressive leadership skills.

Several companies of Spartans were created from colonial children who had been orphaned during the course of the war. These child soldiers were to be clad in the extremely advanced Semi-Powered Infiltration (SPI) armor, which incorporated improvements gleaned directly from Covenant technology.

PROMETHEUS AND TORPEDO
The very first company of Spartan-IIIs, Alpha Company, began training in December 2531. Although this company successfully participated in a number of dangerous operations, nearly all of its Spartans were lost during Operation: PROMETHEUS. The extreme-risk mission sent the Spartan-IIIs to a Covenant shipyard on the asteroid K7-49, where they destroyed the site's plasma reactors, crippling the Covenant's naval efforts on the front lines.

In July 2537, Beta Company was formed from the second wave of Spartan-IIIs. They would go on to complete a number of missions, eventually culminating in TORPEDO: the destruction of a vast Covenant fuel refinery on Pegasi Delta. The refinery was critical to the Covenant's dominance in that region. The mission, though successful, claimed the lives of nearly all members of Beta except for Tom-B292 and Lucy-B091, who would return to SPARTAN-III, helping to train the companies that were to follow.

GAMMA COMPANY
In July 2544, Gamma Company was activated. This time, as well as the standard Spartan-III biological augmentations, mutagenic enhancements were introduced. These illegal genetic modifications gave the Gamma Company Spartans more endurance and aggression under extreme stress, but required them to take a stabilizing drug for the rest of their lives.

While most of Gamma Company was deployed in 2552, making them the last such company to serve in the war, a number remained behind for highly-specialized training. This would prove fortuitous for the UNSC at the end of the war, as the Covenant eventually made their way to Onyx in search of the Forerunner secrets the planet held.

SET APART
The bulk of the Spartans in these three companies were used in large-scale assaults on Covenant targets—missions that would claim the vast majority of their lives. A handful from each company, however, were secretly held back for incorporation into covert Special Warfare teams or as part of the HEADHUNTERS initiative. Outfitted with Mjolnir armor similar to the Spartan-IIs, these spec-ops Spartan-IIIs would play significant roles during the remainder of the war—the most renowned being those of Noble Team.

SPI ARMOR

DESIGNATION: Semi-Powered Infiltration Armor
USED BY: SPARTAN-III
MANUFACTURER: The Watershed Division
DESIGN LEAD: Ruk Ariaustin
PRODUCTION: Currahee Special Assembly Plant 2, Onyx
IOC: 1QFY39
TOTAL NUMBER OF SYSTEMS: 2000+

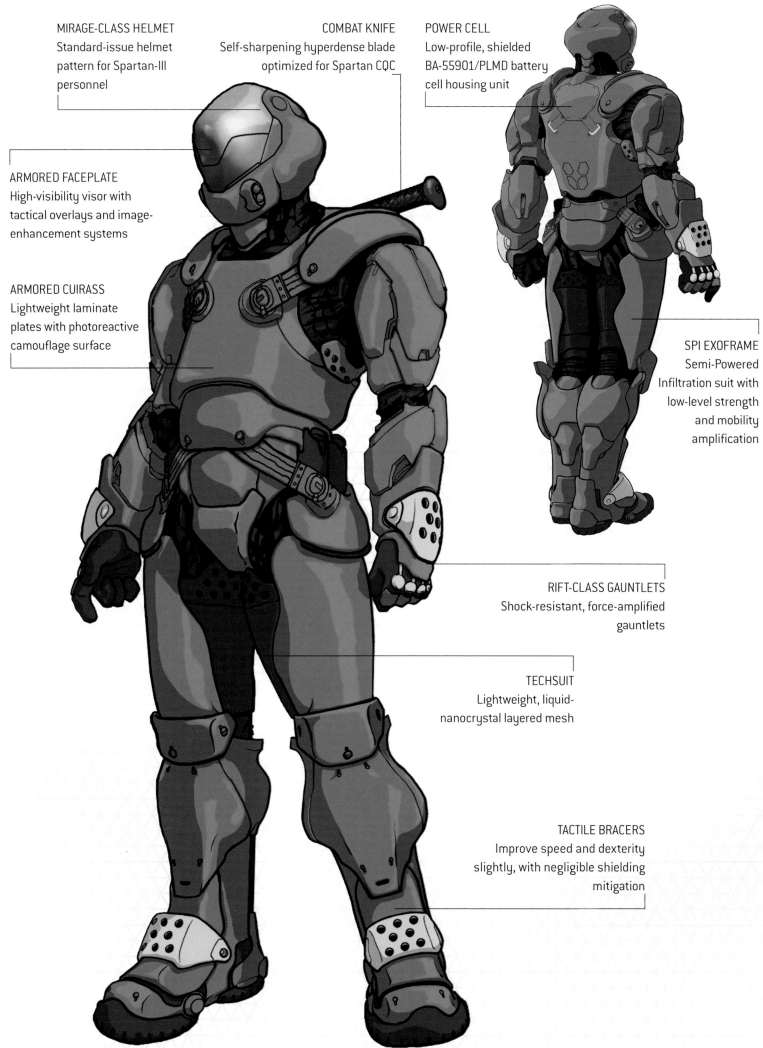

MIRAGE-CLASS HELMET
Standard-issue helmet pattern for Spartan-III personnel

COMBAT KNIFE
Self-sharpening hyperdense blade optimized for Spartan CQC

POWER CELL
Low-profile, shielded BA-55901/PLMD battery cell housing unit

ARMORED FACEPLATE
High-visibility visor with tactical overlays and image-enhancement systems

ARMORED CUIRASS
Lightweight laminate plates with photoreactive camouflage surface

SPI EXOFRAME
Semi-Powered Infiltration suit with low-level strength and mobility amplification

RIFT-CLASS GAUNTLETS
Shock-resistant, force-amplified gauntlets

TECHSUIT
Lightweight, liquid-nanocrystal layered mesh

TACTILE BRACERS
Improve speed and dexterity slightly, with negligible shielding mitigation

Spartan-IIIs were created for high-risk, high-value military operations expected to result in massive casualties— missions often referred to as 'meat grinders.' ONI would deploy entire companies of Spartans directly at major Covenant threats. Their whole lives in the program were designed to prepare them for the short window of a mission which they had little chance of surviving. Most of these heroic soldiers were only in their early teens.

Jean-Sébastien Rossbach

UNDER SIEGE

The period between the implementation of the Cole Protocol and the end of the war is often referred to as the Siege of the Inner Colonies. For humanity, this was a time of silent dread, frequently punctuated by the Covenant's ruthless eradication of a colony. Although human worlds were not being destroyed at the pace they had been earlier in the war, there was still little to stop the Covenant's steady advance through human territory.

Jean-Sébastien Rossbach

SIGMA OCTANUS IV

Although there were a handful of victories for humanity during the Siege of the Inner Colonies, these were only minor setbacks in the Covenant's campaign. Propaganda and willful ignorance kept the innermost colonies, and in particular the Sol system, detached from the actual horrors taking place—but for those who grasped the scale of the threat, the extinction of mankind seemed to be guaranteed.

On July 17, 2552, Covenant scouting vessels struck the lush, jungle colony of Sigma Octanus IV. Only a single human ship, the UNSC *Iroquois*, survived the initial attack. It was here that Commander Jacob Keyes displayed his naval skills by conducting one of the most impressive tactical maneuvers in UNSC history: the ploy that came to be known as the 'Keyes Loop.'

Keyes was no stranger to naval combat and already had decades of experience; his narrow but brilliant victory in this skirmish would finally gain him fame and the rank of captain. Only hours later, however, the enemy returned, this time bringing immense, invasion-scale numbers in the form of the Covenant's Second Fleet of Solemn Accord.

The Battle of Sigma Octanus IV had begun. Marines and Spartans struck the heart of the Covenant's planetside invasion while the UNSC Navy fought in orbit. The Covenant's specific goals for this colony were revealed when Spartans located a concentration of enemy forces at a museum in the

IROQUOIS (DD-906)

CLASS: *Halberd*-class Destroyer
LENGTH: 485 meters
PRIMARY ARMAMENT: 14B11R2 MAC Battery
KEEL LAID: 2551
LAUNCHED: 2552
CAPTAIN: Commander Jacob Keyes
MOTTO: *Alea Iacta Est*

ADVANCED SENSOR ARRAY
Mk 45 long-range fire director

BRIDGE
Late war ε-pattern layout,
increased field of view

FUSION DRIVES
Four primary and four secondary
high-thrust fusion drives

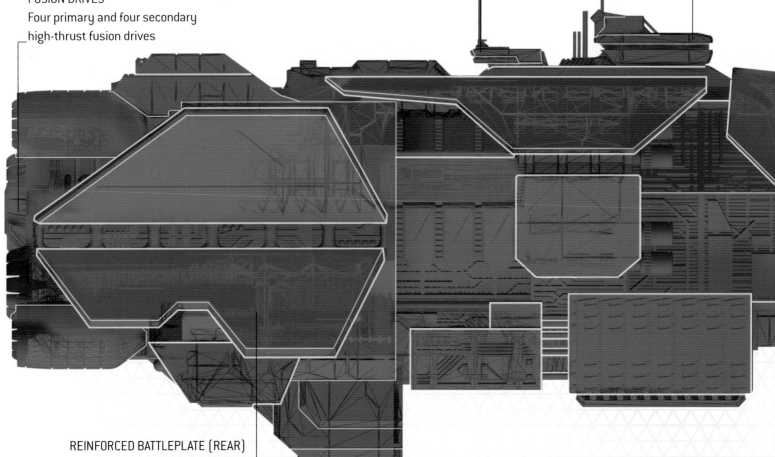

REINFORCED BATTLEPLATE (REAR)
Armored screens fitted to protect fusion
drives and slipspace core

city of Côte d'Azur. The aliens were transmitting data from a fossilized stone recovered by human colonists long ago.

Far above the city, a Covenant vessel attempted to capture this data, but was waylaid by Keyes' *Iroquois* before it was acquired. The data was instead collected by the *Iroquois*' crew and, amazingly, what was left of the Second Fleet of Solemn Accord fled from the remaining UNSC forces.

The unexpected victory at Sigma Octanus IV came at a critical time in the war, but it would be weeks before the true implications were revealed. Hidden within the data the aliens had so desperately sought were the coordinates for an ancient weapon far beyond the power of anything the humans or the Covenant possessed—as well as a secret that would forever change the course of the war.

JACOB KEYES
The epitome of loyalty and bravery, Jacob Keyes has had a diverse and unorthodox history of service within the UNSC Navy. Though eventually returning to combat, Keyes spent a number of years serving as an instructor at the Luna OCS (Officer Candidate School) due to injuries sustained on the Meriwether Lewis. Before this, he even served as military escort for Catherine Halsey, in a heavily classified scouting operation for SPARTAN-II candidates.

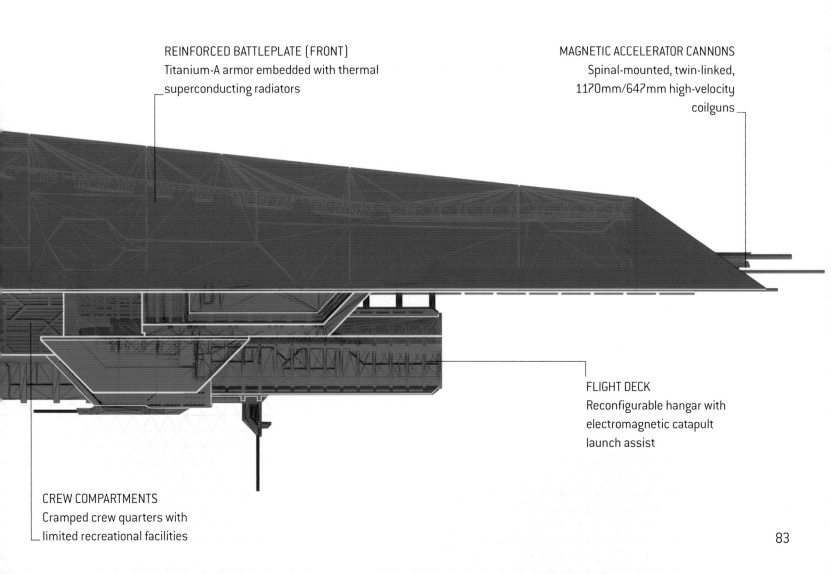

REINFORCED BATTLEPLATE (FRONT)
Titanium-A armor embedded with thermal superconducting radiators

MAGNETIC ACCELERATOR CANNONS
Spinal-mounted, twin-linked, 1170mm/647mm high-velocity coilguns

FLIGHT DECK
Reconfigurable hangar with electromagnetic catapult launch assist

CREW COMPARTMENTS
Cramped crew quarters with limited recreational facilities

END OF THE
WAR

With only a few dozen colonies remaining, ONI believed it was a matter of months, if not weeks, before the Covenant arrived at Reach—and then Earth would be next on the list. To prevent this, ONI planned for Spartans to strike at the heart of the Covenant, abduct one of their Prophets, and hold them hostage, hoping to force the enemy into a truce. This plan was called Operation: RED FLAG.

Over the course of the war the Spartans had become legendary. From their actions were spun tales of valor and glory. They were icons of hope, constantly defying reason and logic, and gaining victory over innumerable threats. Among the Spartans, one had stood above the rest in renown and accomplishment: Master Chief Petty Officer John-117. He would become the central figure in the design of RED FLAG, carrying its critical mission asset deep into enemy territory.

Born on the rebellion-embroiled colony of Eridanus II in 2511, John was integrated into the SPARTAN-II program at the age of six. While his training and augmentation were not unique among his peers, he gained a reputation among them as a born leader, spearheading a number of operations at an impressively young age. Shortly after the war began he rose to the rank of Master Chief Petty Officer, a title which would become synonymous with him.

Prior to RED FLAG, John had fought in over 200 individual military engagements, both on the ground and in space. He had been awarded every single major medal in combat except for Prisoner of War; even among the legendary Spartans, he was without equal. For this reason, he was selected to be a vital component in the RED FLAG operation.

The Chief would be given Cortana, an incredibly advanced AI construct capable of subverting and infiltrating Covenant systems. The information she possessed was crucial for humanity's victory, and the Chief would be her protector.

The fate of the war would rest on their shoulders.

THE FALL OF REACH

After nearly three decades of bloodshed, defending the Inner Colony world of Reach was of crucial importance. If this last bastion of military power fell, there would be little left to protect Earth and the colonies of Sol. Consequently, when the Covenant finally laid siege to Reach, the UNSC marshaled all its remaining forces and prepared to fight to the bitter end.

Leonid Kozienko

WINTER CONTINGENCY

On July 23, 2552, Covenant scouting parties were first detected on the planet Reach by Army fireteams investigating a downed communications relay near the settlement of Visegrád. WINTER CONTINGENCY went into effect immediately: a standing security protocol to be triggered should the Covenant ever infiltrate Reach. With the relay compromised, the colony was cut off from contact with the rest of human-controlled space.

Shortly after this initial security breach, a number of small Covenant vessels managed to penetrate Reach's outer defenses, constructing a vast stealth canopy along the Szurdok Ridge to hide their presence. The UNSC struck this site with great force, revealing a series of teleportation spires for ferrying Covenant troops and supplies from the enemy's immense supercarrier *Long Night of Solace*. The UNSC then initiated Operation: UPPER CUT—a covert mission to destroy the vessel in order to buy ONI time to execute RED FLAG.

UPPER CUT

Already involved in much of what had occurred earlier on Reach, the Spartan-III fireteam known as Noble was critical in the execution of UPPER CUT. Led by the battle-hardened Carter-A259, Noble consisted of tactical and logistics specialist Kat-B320, forward recon scout Jun-A266, close-quarters combatant Emile-A239, and the only Spartan-II of the squad, Jorge-052. A sixth member of the team was added shortly before the Covenant's invasion, and this individual—Spartan-B312, also known as Noble Six—would prove indispensable in the final hours of the battle.

Noble Team was sent to break the Covenant's hold on a launch facility at Farkas Lake. Hidden there were Sabre orbital fighters essential to UPPER CUT. Having taken back the launch site, Noble Six and Jorge-052 led a Sabre squadron into orbit, infiltrating and subverting a Covenant corvette called *Ardent Prayer*. This enemy ship was used to carry a rigged UNSC slipspace drive that, when activated, destroyed *Long Night of Solace*, though at the cost of Jorge-052's life. Miraculously, Noble Six survived, returning to Reach's surface and making his way to the heavily Covenant-occupied city of New Alexandria.

RED FLAG

ONI then initiated RED FLAG. Nearly all surviving Spartan-II super-soldiers had been recalled from other fronts in the war, and a *Halcyon*-class cruiser, the *Pillar of Autumn*, had been refitted as a heavily armored warship. This ship was to be commanded by Captain Jacob Keyes, who was just returning from the battle at Sigma Octanus IV.

The key component of the mission was an artificial intelligence built by Doctor Halsey: Cortana. The AI would be used by a Spartan strike team to infiltrate a Covenant capital ship and capture one of the enemy's leaders, in order to force a truce and bring an end to the war.

Upon extraction from New Alexandria, the surviving Spartans of Noble were immediately sent to Sword Base, an ONI military outpost located in a remote ice shelf called Babd Catha. Here, Halsey and her team were exploring an immense and mysterious Forerunner artifact: a crashed ship, buried under the ice for thousands of years. Using Cortana, Halsey had managed to retrieve navigation data from the ancient vessel—data that ONI hoped would be critical to turning the tide against the Covenant.

LAST STAND

When Noble Team reached Sword Base, Halsey revealed their final mission: to deliver Cortana and her data to the UNSC *Pillar of Autumn*. Despite the overwhelming battle raging in orbit, the ship had withdrawn to Aszód, a barren, unpopulated territory on Reach's surface. Noble Six rendezvoused successfully with Captain Keyes, holding off Covenant forces long enough for the *Pillar of Autumn* to escape with Cortana. This act of valor would prove to be the end of Noble Team, but the beginning of humanity's final hope.

LAST STAND

Although pockets of resistance continued after August 30, 2552, this date would informally mark the end of the fight for Reach. With the full weight of the largest military invasion of the war, the Covenant brutally pummeled Reach, reducing most of its surface to smoldering glass and ash. Nevertheless, amid the tragedy and massive loss of life, there was a single ray of hope.

The Spartans of Noble Team, among others, had heroically sacrificed their lives in defense of the world. What remained of Noble in these final hours charged through the besieged ship-breaker yards of Aszód and delivered a critical package to Captain Jacob Keyes and the UNSC *Pillar of Autumn*. This effort allowed Cortana to escape from Reach, and with her, the key to humanity's survival.

Leonid Kozienko

ESCAPE FROM REACH

With Reach's surface battered by the Covenant's brutal attack, and the local naval forces fighting impossible odds, ONI believed Operation: RED FLAG was the only remaining hope for humanity. UNSC *Pillar of Autumn*, commanded by Captain Jacob Keyes and carrying nearly all remaining Spartan-II soldiers, was ordered to intercept a Covenant vessel and capture one of their leaders, forcing a ceasefire. During the initial skirmish, the mission was jeopardized and Keyes was forced to abort RED FLAG. Although humanity's best hope at ending the war had failed, it led to their greatest discovery: Halo.

PILLAR OF AUTUMN

Leonid Kozienko

While Noble Team was fighting on the ground, another battle raged in the sky above. Hours before the *Autumn* retrieved Cortana at Aszód, two problems emerged that overshadowed even the loss of Reach. First, the generators that powered Reach's orbital guns had been located by the Covenant. If the generators were destroyed, the UNSC naval force would be quickly crushed, sealing the planet's fate and leaving only a handful of ships to defend Earth. Second, the UNSC *Circumference*, docked at the orbital Gamma Station, was unable to initiate Cole Protocol. If the Covenant accessed *Circumference*, Earth's location would be compromised and humanity would lose the war.

Captain Keyes recognized the severity of these threats and delayed RED FLAG in the hope that his ship's crew could both save the planet's orbital guns and prevent Earth's location from falling into Covenant hands. The Spartan-IIs were divided into two highly mobile strike teams: Blue Team was sent to Gamma Station to secure the *Circumference* and Red Team was sent to the generators on the planet's surface.

Both of these missions resulted in heavy casualties—more Spartan-II deaths than in any prior operation in the war. Leading Blue Team, the Master Chief managed to secure the *Circumference*'s data from the Covenant, narrowly escaping to the *Autumn*. Red Team was not so fortunate. Led by Frederic-104, the team's dropship was shot down on entry, the crash claiming the lives of several Spartans. Those who survived landfall heroically defended the generators, but were ultimately forced out when the Covenant overwhelmed the facility with a massive army.

The abandonment of the generators only came after it was clear Reach's defenses had already been crushed by the Covenant. Nevertheless, what remained of Red Team would not give up the fight. With new orders to escort Doctor Catherine Halsey and Vice Admiral Danforth Whitcomb off the planet, the team headed to ONI's Castle Base, hidden below Menachite Mountain.

FUSION DRIVE
Mark II Hanley-Messer DFR sublight, designed for bulk maneuvering rather than speed

POINT DEFENSE GUNS
Agile, synchronously targeting M910 Rampart 50mm for flank coverage

HANGARS
Utilized for quick, *ad hoc* troop deployment via Pelican and Albatross dropships

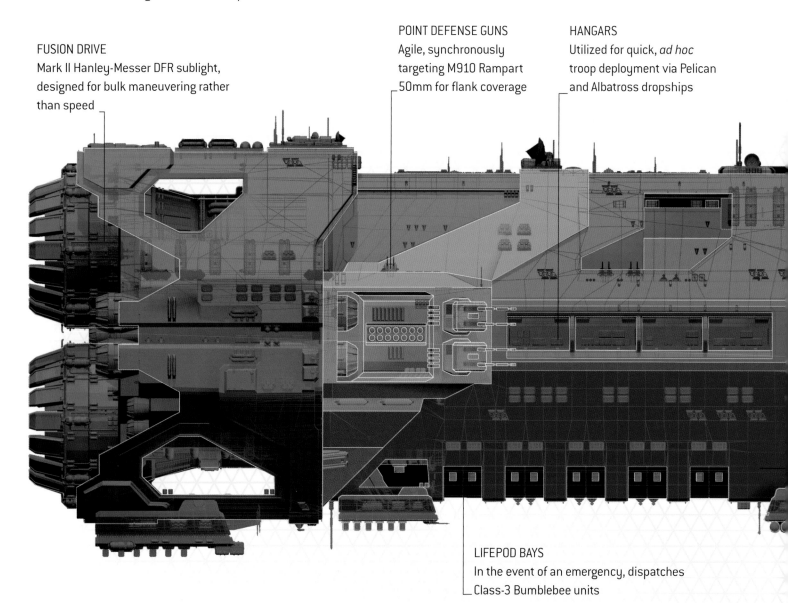

LIFEPOD BAYS
In the event of an emergency, dispatches Class-3 Bumblebee units

ESCAPE

As the planet's surface descended into chaos, and contact was lost with Red Team, Captain Keyes decided to abort RED FLAG. The *Pillar of Autumn* now carried the Master Chief and Cortana, and the AI held the Forerunner navigation data yielded from Halsey's research on Reach—far too significant to risk capture. Following the Cole Protocol, Keyes ordered Cortana to take the ship on a random course safely away from Reach, in order to assess damages and elude their Covenant pursuers.

It was here that the war took a pivotal turn. Cortana combined the data recovered by the *Iroquois* from Sigma Octanus IV with the navigation framework she had extracted from the Forerunner vessel buried on Reach, and produced a seemingly random grouping of coordinates. Holding onto the narrowest margin of hope and with the destruction of Reach at their back, Cortana took the *Pillar of Autumn* and its crew into the depths of slipspace, to a remote and unexplored star system.

CORTANA

Built using the brain of her own flash-clone, Catherine Halsey violated a number of laws in the creation of Cortana, attempting to yield the most advanced and unique AI ever created by humanity. Cortana was designed to infiltrate Covenant security systems, guiding a highly mobile Spartan strike team deep enough behind enemy lines to capture one of their leaders and ultimately broker a truce.

Unlike 'dumb AIs' which limited their focus to a single field, Cortana and all other 'smart AIs' operated virtually the same as humans, except for one fatal side effect. Due to rampancy, a dangerous cognitive instability generally experienced after seven years, smart AIs were preemptively terminated by the UNSC at that point. The burden of a definitive, predetermined mortality was often haunting for the AIs forced to bear it.

MAGNETIC ACCELERATOR CANNON
Spinal-mounted, legacy variant of a Mark II coilgun

BRIDGE
Though somewhat exposed to weapon fire, the command deck is positioned to quickly survey the battle

BATTLEPLATE
Titanium-A armor exterior with honeycomb reinforcement, designed to take a beating

PILLAR OF AUTUMN (C-709)
CLASS: *Halcyon*-class Light Cruiser
LENGTH: 1,171 meters
PRIMARY ARMAMENT: 56A2D4 MAC
KEEL LAID: 2507
LAUNCHED: 2510
CAPTAIN: Captain Jacob Keyes
MOTTO: *Ad Arcendam Hostium*

BATTLE FOR ALPHA HALO

On September 19, 2552, several weeks since their departure from Reach, the *Pillar of Autumn* emerged from slipspace in the remote Soell system. As they headed toward the enormous gas giant known as Threshold, the *Autumn*'s crew made an extraordinary discovery. Hidden in a stable position between the planet and its rocky moon, Basis, was a massive artificial ringworld 10,000 kilometers in diameter.

This was Alpha Halo, the very same installation that Bornstellar had committed to 343 Guilty Spark's care 100,000 years earlier. This Halo would now be the stage for one of the final battles of the Covenant War, revealing mysteries kept hidden for eons.

Leonid Kozienko

ARRIVAL

Approaching the ring aboard the heavily damaged *Autumn*, Captain Keyes and Cortana quickly discovered that the Covenant had followed them from Reach. After sending the Master Chief and Cortana to the ringworld's surface in an effort to ensure the AI's safety, Keyes attempted to land the *Autumn* on Halo, despite the extremely high risk involved in such a maneuver.

The *Autumn* successfully touched down, but Keyes and his command crew were abducted by the Covenant and brought aboard their battlecruiser *Truth and Reconciliation*. In response, the Chief and Cortana led a strike force into the heart of the enemy ship and rescued the captain. While captive, Keyes learned that Halo was not just an artificial world, but an unimaginably powerful weapon.

THE FLOOD UNLEASHED

The Chief and Cortana managed to secure the installation's control room against Covenant forces, but their victory was short-lived. Communication with Keyes and a squad of marines, who were attempting to access a weapon cache on the ring, had suddenly been lost. During the Covenant's search for Halo's secrets, they had unwittingly released Flood specimens, previously locked away for research on the installation. The parasite's escape now placed the entire galaxy in peril.

Attempting to track down Keyes and his team, the Chief came in contact with the installation's monitor, 343 Guilty Spark. Spark explained to the Spartan the severity of the Flood threat and led the Chief to Halo's Library, where they managed to secure the ring's Activation Index—the key to firing Halo and stopping the Flood. With the Index in possession, the Spartan returned to the control room alongside the monitor, intent on activating Halo to stop the parasite from escaping.

The Chief had been acting on the assumption that firing Halo would kill the Flood—but he was not aware that the installation was designed to exterminate all sentient life in the galaxy. When Spark attempted to activate the ring, Cortana prevented him and stole the Index, placing both her and the Chief at odds with the Forerunner monitor. Escaping the control room, the two recognized that the only way to end the threat was to destroy the ring.

DESTRUCTION

This plan could only be achieved by destroying the *Pillar of Autumn*, which would in turn require finding Captain Keyes and his command codes. The Chief and Cortana located his signal, but discovered that he had been assimilated by the Flood. They retrieved his command neural interface from what was left of his body, using it to destabilize the *Autumn*'s fusion engines and destroy Alpha Halo—despite Guilty Spark's desperate efforts to stop them.

The Master Chief and Cortana narrowly escaped the ring's destruction on one of the *Autumn*'s Longsword bombers, believing themselves to be the only survivors. Unbeknownst to them, however, Spark had also fled to safety, finding sanctuary on a Forerunner gas mine orbiting Threshold.

ALPHA HALO
Known as Installation 04, the massive fortress world called Alpha Halo was monitored by 343 Guilty Spark. It would be the site of a watershed discovery for humanity—and a glimmer of hope against the marauding Covenant war machine.

UNYIELDING HIEROPHANT

Having escaped Halo's devastation, the Chief and Cortana discovered a human dropship within the debris that remained, containing a handful of survivors from the *Pillar of Autumn*, including the gritty Marine veteran Sergeant Avery Johnson.

ASCENDANT JUSTICE

Recognizing that their only way back to human space was by acquiring a slipspace-capable vessel, the Chief led these survivors against the Covenant carrier *Ascendant Justice*. This flagship was commanding a scouting fleet sent from the Covenant's homeworld, High Charity. The Covenant were unprepared for the Chief's daring assault; aided by Cortana, the small group of humans infiltrated *Ascendant Justice* and neutralized its crew.

Cortana brought the humans back to Reach in the stolen vessel on September 23, 2552. They found the planet in ruins, but detected a signal, which the Chief recognized as originating from Red Team. Somehow a remnant of Spartans had miraculously survived Reach's devastation.

Deploying stealthily from *Ascendant Justice*, the Chief led a small team to recover the remaining members of Red Team, who were guarding Vice Admiral Whitcomb and Doctor Halsey. While escaping the planet, however, the Spartans were greeted by chilling news: despite their extraordinary sacrifices, the Covenant had somehow discovered the location of Earth, and were preparing an enormous fleet to assault it.

With few viable destinations available, they fled to the Eridanus system in order to make repairs. In this system was a hidden rebel base, the same one used by the rebel Colonel Watts years earlier. Unexpectedly, the Covenant followed them there and laid siege to the base, forcing the humans to flee into slipspace.

BETRAYAL

Yet some of these survivors did not share the same goal. While the Spartans were considering options for stopping the Covenant's imminent invasion of Earth, Halsey was preoccupied with something she had discovered at Castle Base before they fled the planet. In what seemed to be an act of betrayal, Halsey sedated and abducted Spartan Kelly-087, stealing one of the rebel transports and abandoning the group without any warning. This act, despite eventually unlocking one of humanity's greatest Forerunner discoveries, would ultimately come to haunt Halsey, effectively making her a war criminal.

The Master Chief, Cortana, and the others who managed to escape from Eridanus, devised a plan to halt the Covenant's invasion of Earth. Striking at the heart of an enormous command-and-control station called Unyielding Hierophant, they would destroy the many fleets that it serviced, delaying the Covenant's efforts to assault Earth.

Using an enemy dropship to insert a Spartan strike team, the Chief and the rest of Blue Team infiltrated Hierophant's vast interior and successfully completed their mission. Almost all of the nearby ships were consumed in the violent conflagration that engulfed Unyielding Hierophant, leaving only a handful to limp back to High Charity. For a time, the invasion of Earth had been postponed.

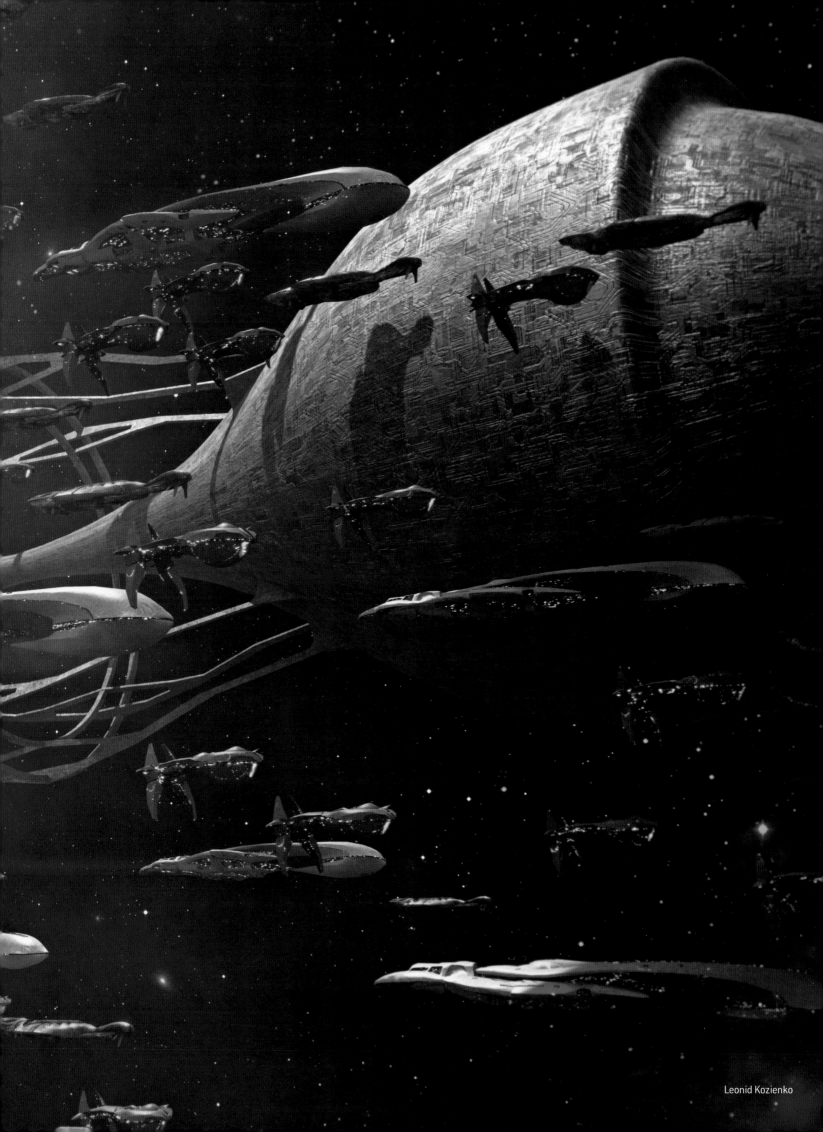

Leonid Kozienko

ASSAULT ON EARTH

Though the Covenant's efforts to deal a death blow to humanity were momentarily averted with the destruction of Unyielding Hierophant, little could stop their plans from being realized. Humanity would have to muster all their remaining forces in their home system and prepare for the desperate struggle to come. But below the surface of the Earth, another secret that had lain hidden for a hundred thousand years was about to emerge.

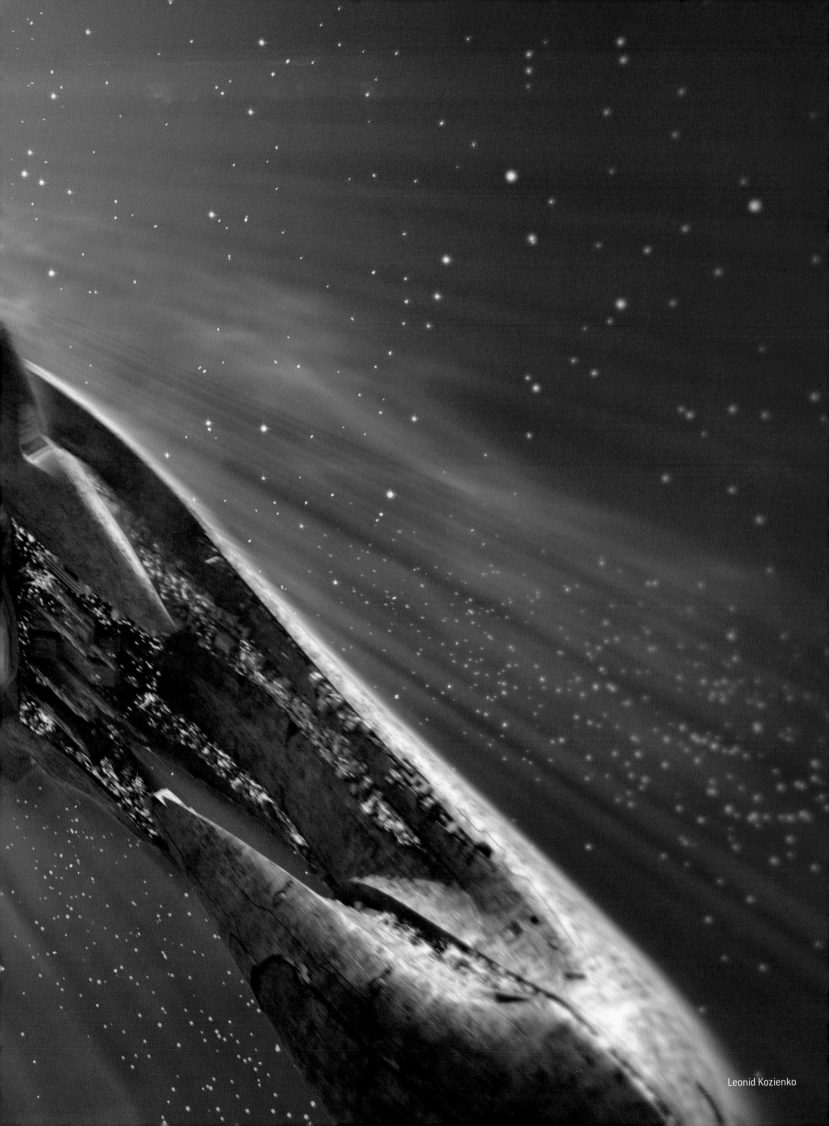

Leonid Kozienko

SUBTERFUGE

The destruction of Unyielding Hierophant was a major setback for the High Prophet of Truth, who had remained in power during the war alongside the High Prophets Regret and Mercy—the very same San'Shyuum who had risen to power shortly after the discovery of humanity almost three decades earlier. Not only had Truth intended to seize control of Earth, but he had also secretly plotted a coup against the Sangheili.

The Sangheili would be replaced by the Jiralhanae—the Brutes—under the leadership of the chieftain known as Tartarus. He would be given command of the entire Covenant military by the Prophet. Having for some time questioned the Sangheili's loyalty, Truth believed this transition was now necessary to secure his power as the Covenant finally moved to activate Halo.

Unbeknownst to Truth, however, the High Prophet of Regret had his own plans. Regret had discovered the location of Earth while ransacking the defeated human colony of Meridian a year earlier. The Prophet was unaware that Earth was the human homeworld, but did know that buried there was a portal leading to the Ark: the location from which all Halo installations could be activated. Taking the Fleet of Sacred Consecration, a meager fifteen vessels in total, the High Prophet of Regret set out to seize this planet and activate the portal for himself.

DEFENSE OF EARTH

Only a few days before Regret's arrival on October 20, 2552, the Master Chief, Cortana, and the others who survived their mission finally returned to Earth, providing the UNSC with insight into the Covenant's plans. Fleet Admiral Terrence Hood headed Earth's primary defense, the Home Fleet, and the vast network of orbital weapons that protected the planet. When the Covenant struck, the Chief and Cortana were stationed on the orbiting weapon platform Cairo Station, which allowed them to assault and destroy the Covenant fleet's second carrier, *Day of Jubilation*.

Also aboard Cairo were Sergeant Avery Johnson, and Commander Miranda Keyes of UNSC *In Amber Clad*— daughter of Jacob Keyes, who had sacrificed his life just weeks before on Alpha Halo. The Chief and Cortana, along with Keyes and Johnson, pursued Regret's flagship *Solemn Penance* to the Earth city of New Mombasa.

Regret's military force was desperate to find some method of exposing the portal that they knew lay hidden below the city, but the Forerunner machine continued to elude them and time was running out: the Master Chief, of whom Regret had heard terrible rumors, was approaching his position. Fearing for his life, Regret changed his plans.

The source of the information he had retrieved from Meridian months earlier was a unique Forerunner luminary, which not only revealed the ancient portal's location on Earth, but also the locations of the remaining Halo ringworlds. Regret set a course for Delta Halo.

THE RIFT

The Prophet's ship entered slipspace directly above New Mombasa, tearing open a rift across the northern part of the city. He believed this might expose the portal artifact and allow the Covenant ships that remained to continue their mission. The High Prophet of Regret was unaware, however, that in his haste he was followed by the UNSC *In Amber Clad*— carrying not only Commander Keyes and Sergeant Johnson, but also Cortana—and the Master Chief.

THE FIGHT FOR NEW MOMBASA

On October 20, 2552, the High Prophet of Regret's sudden escape in *Solemn Penance* revealed the Forerunner portal artifact's position, buried deep below Earth's surface between the teeming metropolis of New Mombasa and the small industrial town of Voi.

The artifact's existence did not come as a complete surprise to some on Earth. Shortly prior to the Covenant attack, an engineer by the name of Doctor Daniel Endesha had discovered seismic signatures caused by the long-hidden device. During the Covenant siege, ONI learned that this important information had been transmitted to New Mombasa's municipal Superintendent AI, which Endesha had worked closely with. This data would prove critical to human forces as they prepared to defend the site from the Covenant invaders.

ALPHA-NINE

Just before Regret's departure, several squads of Orbital Drop Shock Troopers (ODSTs) had been deployed from the cruiser UNSC *Say My Name*, hoping to breach and seize control of the Prophet's flagship from above. In addition, a single squad of ODSTs had been separated from the pack for another, heavily classified mission: to secure the Superintendent construct, and the data about the hidden Forerunner artifact that it contained. Led by ONI Captain Veronica Dare, the ODST squad called Alpha-Nine was deployed directly into the city.

During the Prophet's violent escape, most of the ODSTs deployed were lost, but Alpha-Nine, though scattered across the city of New Mombasa, managed to survive the slipspace fallout. This squad included Gunnery Sergeant Edward Buck, Corporal Taylor 'Dutch' Miles, Lance Corporal Kojo 'Romeo' Agu, Private First Class Michael 'Mickey' Crespo, and the newest addition, an ODST simply referred to as the Rookie.

Though separated from each other, they eventually reunited and successfully secured their objective: a subroutine of the Superintendent known as 'Vergil,' which had been transmitted into the body of a Covenant Huragok. On October 21, 2552, Alpha-Nine, having survived the Covenant siege of New Mombasa, brought the Huragok back to an ONI space station for evaluation.

MUTINY

As dawn broke over New Mombasa, more Covenant ships arrived and began to excavate the artifact. However, the Covenant did not emerge from this battle unscathed. The High Prophet of Truth had triggered his planned revolt against the Sangheili. Jiralhanae within Regret's fleet were ordered to wrest control from the Sangheili; and even before Regret's assault carrier took flight from New Mombasa, Jiralhanae were rioting in Covenant vessels and executing Sangheili in the streets of the city.

Despite incredible odds, ONI's efforts to secure Vergil in the besieged city of New Mombasa were successful. Alpha-Nine proved their indelible grit and fortitude, true to the form of the Orbital Drop Shock Troopers. As a division of the Marines, the ODST had played a key role throughout the war, its troopers deployed by way of drop pods from capital ships high above the atmosphere. This ferocious audacity earned the ODST the moniker of 'Helljumpers,' and despite them falling short of being Spartans, such fearless tactics and unwavering boldness struck fear into the heart of the Covenant.

Leonid Kozienko

BATTLE FOR DELTA HALO

When the High Prophet of Regret fled from Earth, he took *Solemn Penance* directly to Delta Halo. He hoped to activate the Array and usher the Covenant into divinity, as had been prophesied by their kind for centuries. Blinded by the prospect of glory, the Prophet was not mindful of the threat that the pursuing UNSC *In Amber Clad* posed, carrying the Master Chief, the very Spartan who had pursued him across New Mombasa. Neither party was aware that the same Gravemind that had led the Flood against the Forerunners a hundred millennia ago lurked below the surface of this newly discovered ringworld—biding its time until someone returned, bringing vessels fit to carry the Flood out into the galaxy once more.

Leonid Kozienko

THE ARBITER

After the destruction of Alpha Halo, Thel 'Vadamee, the Sangheili commander whose fleets had occupied the installation, was blamed for the calamity. Rather than execute 'Vadamee , the High Prophets instead named him Arbiter—an ancient title once held in honor, but now considered a mark of shame. He would serve as the Will of the Prophets until his death.

The Arbiter was immediately sent to eradicate a Sangheili-led rebellion at a Forerunner gas mine near Alpha Halo. Here he encountered an Oracle—343 Guilty Spark of the destroyed ring. The Forerunner monitor would now become a captive of the Prophet leadership aboard High Charity as they made their way to Delta Halo to follow Regret.

DEATH OF A HIERARCH

Solemn Penance arrived on the new ringworld, Delta Halo, on November 3, 2552, pursued by the Master Chief and Cortana aboard the UNSC *In Amber Clad*. Commander Miranda Keyes sent the Chief to hunt down and terminate Regret in one of the Halo's temple sites, isolated at the center of a lake. Before he could complete this task, however, the Covenant's Holy City of High Charity and all that remained of their massive fleet arrived at the ring. Although the Chief succeeded in assassinating Regret, the High Prophet of Truth ordered the immediate destruction of the temple, sending the Spartan plunging into the murky depths of the lake.

GREAT SCHISM

Recognizing the importance of securing Delta Halo's Index, the key to activating the ring, Keyes and Sergeant Avery Johnson hurried to the ring's Library. The Arbiter had also been sent by Truth and Mercy to secure the same prize. The Arbiter managed to stop the humans and retrieve the Index, but he was unexpectedly betrayed by the Prophet of Truth's leading Jiralhanae, Tartarus.

This move signaled the beginning of the Covenant civil war, formally known as the Great Schism. Following Truth's secret coup among the ships surrounding Earth, he had now ordered a change in High Charity's Honor Guard, replacing Elites with Brutes and throwing the Covenant into chaos.

THE GRAVEMIND

Tartarus sent the Arbiter plummeting into the lower reaches of the Library, where the Sangheili encountered the Gravemind, the monstrous Flood intelligence that had waged war against the Forerunners ages earlier. The Gravemind

HALO RING

DESIGNATION: Installation 05
MONITOR: 2401 Penitent Tangent
STAR SYSTEM: Coelest
GRAVITY ANCHOR: Substance
DIAMETER: 10,000 kilometers
WIDTH: 318 kilometers
GRAVITY: 1.04 G
ATMOSPHERE: 1.01 (N2, O2)

had also captured the Master Chief, but rather than seeking to infect its two captives, it recognized a more serious threat: Halo's activation would prevent it from escaping the installation.

To stop the Covenant from firing Halo, the Gravemind revealed the truth about the rings to the Arbiter. It then sent the Master Chief to High Charity and the Arbiter to Delta Halo's control room, in order to secure the Index and prevent Halo's activation.

As the Master Chief and Cortana fought through High Charity to take back the Index, a horrifying discovery was made. During its incursions on Delta Halo, the UNSC *In Amber Clad* had been taken over by the Flood and the ship had infiltrated High Charity's defenses, now placing the entire galaxy at risk.

When the Chief failed to reach the Index before Tartarus whisked it away to Delta Halo, Cortana was faced with a difficult decision. She would have to part with the Chief in order to make sure that Delta Halo didn't activate. As the Spartan followed the fleeing High Prophet of Truth to the Forerunner dreadnought, Cortana would stay behind. Were Delta Halo to fire, Cortana could use the fusion reactors of the now crashed *In Amber Clad* to destroy High Charity, the ring, and the perilous Flood outbreak.

RACE FOR THE ARK

Working with the humans on Delta Halo's surface, the Arbiter managed to kill Tartarus and prevent the ring's activation. This act, however, tripped a fail-safe mechanism, placing all remaining Halo rings in a precarious standby mode. They could now only be activated from the Ark.

Meanwhile, within High Charity, the Chief had pursued Truth to the Forerunner dreadnought at the center of the city. Abandoning High Charity to the Flood, Truth lifted the dreadnought free from its historic mooring and led all remaining Covenant fleets back to Earth, where they would use the ancient keyship to activate New Mombasa's portal and reach the Ark. Reluctantly leaving Cortana imprisoned within the Flood-infested High Charity, the Master Chief stowed aboard the dreadnought, following Truth back to Earth.

ARBITER

As the Arbiter, Thel 'Vadam wore segmented armor of a traditional design dating back to before the formation of the Covenant, specific only to this ancient Sangheili class of judge-kings. He would be called the 'Will of the Prophets,' and sent on the most treacherous and deadly missions. His certain death in battle would provide absolution for his former sins.

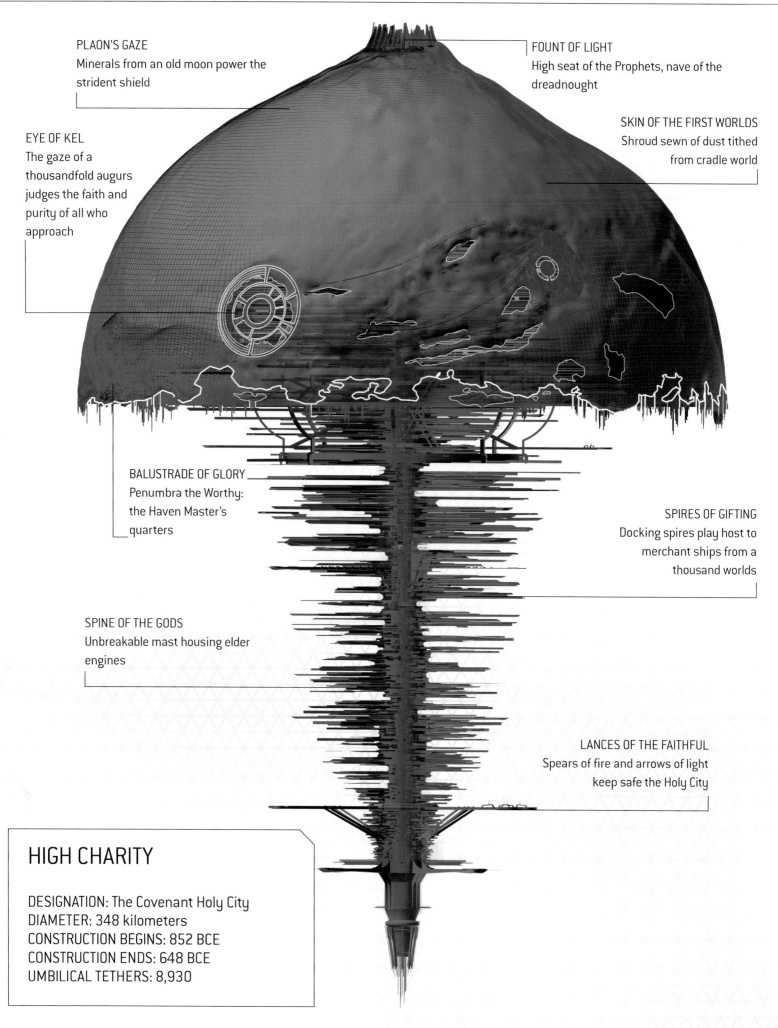

PLAON'S GAZE
Minerals from an old moon power the strident shield

EYE OF KEL
The gaze of a thousandfold augurs judges the faith and purity of all who approach

FOUNT OF LIGHT
High seat of the Prophets, nave of the dreadnought

SKIN OF THE FIRST WORLDS
Shroud sewn of dust tithed from cradle world

BALUSTRADE OF GLORY
Penumbra the Worthy: the Haven Master's quarters

SPIRES OF GIFTING
Docking spires play host to merchant ships from a thousand worlds

SPINE OF THE GODS
Unbreakable mast housing elder engines

LANCES OF THE FAITHFUL
Spears of fire and arrows of light keep safe the Holy City

HIGH CHARITY

DESIGNATION: The Covenant Holy City
DIAMETER: 348 kilometers
CONSTRUCTION BEGINS: 852 BCE
CONSTRUCTION ENDS: 648 BCE
UMBILICAL TETHERS: 8,930

THE ONYX CONFLICT

Shortly before the battle at Delta Halo, hidden artifacts on the mysterious world of Onyx had responded to a remote signal from the destruction of Alpha Halo. This signal revealed that Onyx was, in fact, a Forerunner shield world, drawing the attention of the Covenant—and also Doctor Halsey.

Halsey had abducted Spartan Kelly-087 and traveled to Onyx, hoping to save some of the Spartan-IIIs who had been trained on the classified world, as well as to salvage vital Forerunner technologies. Despite her status as a potential fugitive, Admiral Hood recognized the significance of Halsey's find and deployed Spartan Blue Team to assist immediately.

THE SPHERE
Led by Lieutenant Commander Kurt Ambrose, a group composed of Spartan-IIs, Spartan-IIIs, Halsey, and the battle-hardened drill instructor Franklin Mendez made their way to an immense Forerunner city hidden in a large crater, within a previously restricted area of the planet.

This site held a secret passage into the shield world's core, allowing access to the heart of the installation. At its center was a portal to a slipspace-enclosed Dyson sphere— a vast hollow shell three hundred million kilometers across, containing an artificial sun. The inner surface of this sphere was habitable and terraformed, with an area five hundred million times that of Earth.

But as they moved deeper, attempting to secure the portal to the sphere, others converged on Onyx. The Covenant's Second Fleet of Homogeneous Clarity, followed by UNSC battle group Omicron, and a lone stealth prowler, the *Dusk*, arrived at Onyx. UNSC and Covenant naval forces clashed high above the planet as the Covenant deployed infantry to the surface to follow the Spartans. Pursued right to Onyx's core, the group of humans was waylaid by Covenant forces, and Ambrose was forced to stay behind to stop their enemy while the others entered a portal leading to the Dyson sphere interior.

Once the portal was closed, Ambrose detonated a nuclear weapon to prevent the Covenant's access. It was then that the planetoid began to disintegrate, revealing that it was actually composed almost entirely of Forerunner automated drones called Sentinels—which immediately attacked all those nearby. Both the UNSC battle group and the Covenant fleet were destroyed by these drones, although the *Dusk* escaped to tell the tale. The Spartans and other survivors who accessed the portal, however, found themselves trapped within the immense Dyson sphere interior—with seemingly no way out.

Leonid Kozienko

On November 17, 2552, the High Prophet of Truth's dreadnought finally reached Earth, plowing through what remained of the system's naval defenses. A handful of Covenant ships had been engaged with Earth's forces in the previous weeks, but most of those vessels were preoccupied with the excavation of the massive portal artifact. This incredible machine was the gateway the Librarian had, eons ago, sacrificed her own ship to build, ensuring that one day humanity could return to the Ark.

The Master Chief, who had stowed away aboard the dreadnought, escaped as it entered the atmosphere. Plummeting to the ground, he made landfall in the jungles of Tanzania, narrowly surviving the fall. Transported to the Crow's Nest, a hidden 20th century military base in Kenya, the Chief reunited with Commander Keyes and Sergeant Johnson. The two had recently returned from Delta Halo and were organizing efforts to resist the invasion. Shockingly, the Covenant's civil war led to a tentative alliance with the Arbiter and the Sangheili, as the UNSC poised to stop the Prophet of Truth from getting his prize: access to the Forerunner Ark.

Fleet Admiral Terrence Hood attempted to assault the Prophet's dreadnought with a battle group comprised of frigates, but failed; nothing could stop the ship from reaching its goal. The portal opened and Truth's dreadnought led the remaining Covenant fleet to the Ark.

Leonid Kozienko

THE FLOOD ON EARTH

Mere seconds after the activation of the portal, a single Flood-infested Covenant cruiser arrived on Earth, sent by the Gravemind from High Charity to verify the artifact's location. UNSC forces quickly surrounded the crashed vessel, knowing that the Flood presented an even greater threat to Earth than the Covenant.

Just when it appeared that the humans were unable to contain the Flood, the Sangheili Fleet of Retribution arrived, eliminating the parasite threat by glassing much of eastern Africa. Fleet Commander Rtas 'Vadum brought with him 343 Guilty Spark, who had assisted the Sangheili in quarantining the Flood around High Charity before following the infested cruiser to Earth.

The Fleet of Retribution had pursued this ship because of a mysterious distress beacon it transmitted, alerting all nearby vessels to the peril it represented. Breaking through the debris field, the Master Chief was the first to secure this beacon, which was later revealed to be the remains of a recording by Cortana.

The AI had remained behind on High Charity as it fell to the Flood, and was now trapped there by the Gravemind. In the message, she warned the UNSC of the Gravemind's plans to bring High Charity to Earth, but also hinted that a solution was being prepared—a solution that lay at the other end of the portal that Truth had just activated.

INTO THE ARK

After a somber debate, Hood eventually agreed to allow Commander Keyes to take the *Forward Unto Dawn* and a number of UNSC personnel, including the Master Chief and Sergeant Johnson. They would stow the frigate aboard the Fleet of Retribution's flagship carrier *Shadow of Intent*, following Truth's forces through the portal. What remained of Earth's defenders, though still battling scattered remnants of the Covenant, would entrust their fate to those who had gone to the Ark.

THE FINAL BATTLE

The remaining Covenant fleet gathered above the Ark, preparing to hold off humanity and the rebel Sangheili in order to buy the High Prophet of Truth enough time to activate the Halo Array. Ultimately, it would be a newly-forged Halo ring, hidden deep within the Ark itself, that would spell the end of the threats posed by the Covenant and the Flood.

Leonid Kozienko

ENDGAME

On December 11, 2552, the Fleet of Retribution arrived at the Ark and immediately assaulted the Jiralhanae forces stationed above the installation—the last major vestige of the Covenant navy. Although the Jiralhanae greatly outnumbered the Sangheili, they were outmatched in their knowledge of naval warfare, and Retribution made short work of them. Meanwhile, the Master Chief and the Arbiter were sent to the Ark's surface, accompanied by *Forward Unto Dawn*'s ground forces led by Commander Miranda Keyes and Sergeant Avery Johnson.

Using one of the Ark's map rooms, and with the assistance of 343 Guilty Spark, whose own interests had now aligned with the humans', the Chief and the Arbiter managed to find Truth's location. But as they made their way to stop Truth from activating Halo, the now Flood-dominated city of High Charity suddenly arrived, crashing into the Ark's surface and freeing the parasite.

The Gravemind, yet again sharing a goal with the Master Chief and the Arbiter, assisted them in stopping the High Prophet of Truth from firing the rings.

The Covenant leader ultimately died at the hands of the Arbiter, paying for the deceit and death wrought by his machinations, but only after Truth had claimed the life of Commander Keyes.

A NEW HALO

With the Covenant threat now halted, the Gravemind turned against the humans, gloating about its victory and preparing to unleash the Flood parasite across the galaxy once more. Hidden in the burning forges of the Ark, however, the installation had fashioned yet another Halo, intended to replace the one the Master Chief had destroyed months earlier. As this was the only way to stop the parasite, the Chief and the Arbiter headed to the wreckage of High Charity, battling through its immense and infested interior to find, at last, Cortana, and the key to stopping the Flood.

Cortana still had Alpha Halo's Activation Index, kept safe since she had stolen it months earlier. Igniting the replacement Halo this far removed from the galaxy would allow them to destroy the Flood locally without harming any sentient life in the Milky Way. After securing the Index, the Chief and the Arbiter made their way to the control room of the newly forged Halo installation, alongside Sergeant Avery Johnson.

When the time came to activate it, however, 343 Guilty Spark refused to prematurely fire the installation, as in its unfinished state the activation would completely destroy the Halo superstructure. Due to the urgency of the Flood threat, Johnson attempted to activate the ring anyway, but Spark turned on him, striking him down. The Chief fought back, destroying Guilty Spark and activating Halo.

THE HALO FIRES

Though Johnson perished, the Spartan and the Arbiter managed to narrowly escape aboard *Forward Unto Dawn*. The ring fired directly at the Ark installation, obliterating the Gravemind and its Flood.

The damage done to the Ark destabilized the portal as the *Dawn* passed through it, severing it into two parts. The fore of the ship returned to Earth on December 23, 2552, with the Arbiter aboard.

The aft section, which carried both the Chief and Cortana, was lost during the portal collapse, with no record of its location or status.

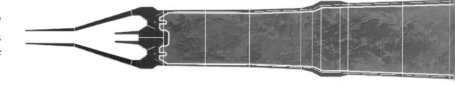

The replacement Halo's activation obliterated the Gravemind and its Flood outbreak, as well as the remaining Covenant forces, ultimately heralding the end of the war. The cost, however, would not be easily forgotten. Countless lives were lost during the conflict and with no trace of the Master Chief, humanity's greatest hero may have been the final sacrifice.

THE ARK

DESIGNATION: Installation 00
STAR SYSTEM: None
STAR(S): Artificial
DAY LENGTH: 35.3 hours (adjustable)
DIAMETER: 127,530 kilometers
MONITOR: 000 Tragic Solitude

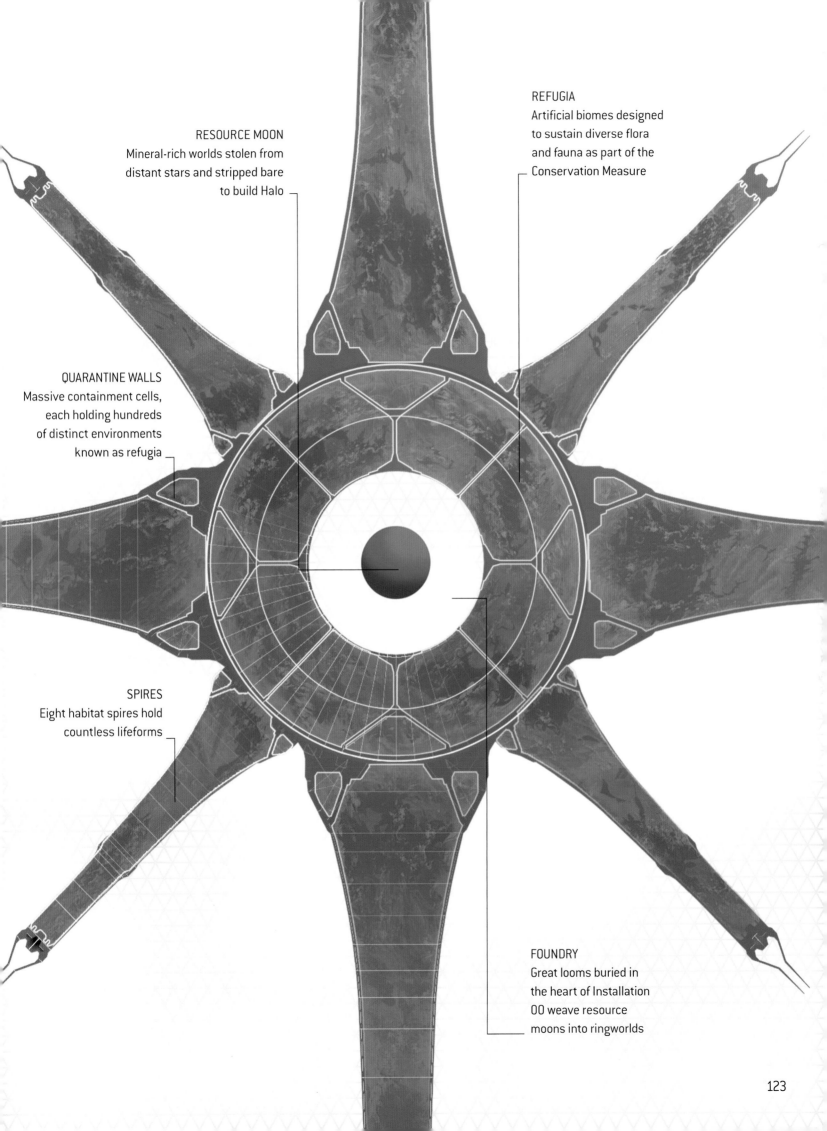

RESOURCE MOON
Mineral-rich worlds stolen from
distant stars and stripped bare
to build Halo

REFUGIA
Artificial biomes designed
to sustain diverse flora
and fauna as part of the
Conservation Measure

QUARANTINE WALLS
Massive containment cells,
each holding hundreds
of distinct environments
known as refugia

SPIRES
Eight habitat spires hold
countless lifeforms

FOUNDRY
Great looms buried in
the heart of Installation
00 weave resource
moons into ringworlds

THE
AFTERMATH

The end of the war was signaled by the return of the UNSC *Forward Unto Dawn* to Earth. The Arbiter emerged as the sole survivor, the Master Chief and Cortana having been lost when the portal from the Ark unexpectedly collapsed, ripping the ship in two. Their fate remained a mystery, but most believed that the Chief had perished in his escape.

When the portal collapsed, the immense artifact that generated it suddenly closed, becoming completely inactive. The pathway to the Ark, the Forerunners' final refuge far outside the Milky Way, was now severed.

Much of the Covenant had been destroyed in High Charity's fall to the Flood. Those who survived the battles at Earth and the Ark, as well as other more remote conflicts, either found their way back to their own worlds or forged new alliances, some of which closely resembled the original Covenant.

The many Elites who returned from the war found that great tension had built on Sanghelios and its outlying colonies. With the discovery that the Forerunners were not gods, but merely an ancient and powerful civilization, some rebelled against more than three thousand years of Covenant religion. Others held onto the traditions of their past, reluctant to abandon the faith that had united their people for so many centuries. Against this backdrop, warring clans and sects sprang up, some seeking political power, others vying for territory.

Despite widespread support for the Arbiter, which stemmed from his central role in bringing an end to the San'Shyuum's tyranny and the Jiralhanae-led revolt, Sanghelios was far from united. Many Sangheili still despised humans, and any alliance or friendship with them was viewed as an insult to their traditions. For this reason, the Arbiter's position of leadership among the Sangheili was constantly threatened by those who saw him as a heretic.

Civil unrest was not restricted to the Sangheili, however. Most of the remaining human worlds united under the banner of peace, working with the UNSC to safeguard their colonies in the years after the war, but a handful were extremely resistant, and sought to declare themselves independent of the Unified Earth Government. Some of these had scarcely survived brutal Covenant attacks, and blamed the UNSC for abandoning them in their hour of need. Others were drawn to the leadership of political idealists, who were anxious to stop any attempts by the UNSC to consolidate Earth's authority. Some worlds even remained outlaw colonies—hostile to the UEG, but open for business to the alien species who had, only months earlier, been waging a war of extermination against them.

In spite of all the uncertainties—colonial unrest, and the remnant factions of the Covenant—secret projects humanity had initiated toward the end of the war would allow the UNSC to regain some level of military power in the months that followed.

THE NEW SPARTANS

Well before the end of the Covenant War, ONI had initiated plans for the SPARTAN-IV program, a huge effort based on the ORION protocols of old. This project targeted consenting adult combat veterans for biological augmentation and use of the newest generation of Mjolnir armor. Spearheaded by Commander Musa-096, who had previously washed out of the SPARTAN-II program due to failed augmentation, a new branch of the military was proposed to UNSC leadership in early 2553: one comprised exclusively of Spartans, and unlike anything the UNSC had envisioned before.

Isaac Hannaford

Working alongside Jun-A266, the sole survivor of Reach's legendary Noble Team, Musa began recruiting personnel from across the existing UNSC branches—soldiers who met extremely high criteria. These impressive men and women were augmented into warriors capable of incredible physical feats. They were outfitted with Mjolnir GEN2 armor, the next evolution of the armor Halsey had fashioned decades earlier.

SARAH PALMER

One of the Spartan branch's first candidates was Sarah Palmer, an ODST of notable skill and bravery. She became a prominent member of the program, and eventually rose to the position of Spartan Commander on the UNSC's flagship *Infinity*.

MASS PRODUCTION

With the branch's growing success, a number of corporations were contracted to produce the costly GEN2 armor used by Spartan-IVs. In May 2553, the Materials Group formed the Damascus Ordnance Commission, bringing in companies such as Lethbridge Industrial, Hannibal Weapon Systems, and Acheron Security to mass produce and refine GEN2 armor systems. This step reflected a huge change—from the relative obscurity of earlier Spartan classes, to the dramatic influence they would now have in human-occupied space.

BROKKR ARMOR MECHANISM—GEN2
Mjolnir armor is difficult to mount directly to a Spartan techsuit without assistance of 'Da Vinci' multi-axis assembly systems such as Material Group's Brokkr.

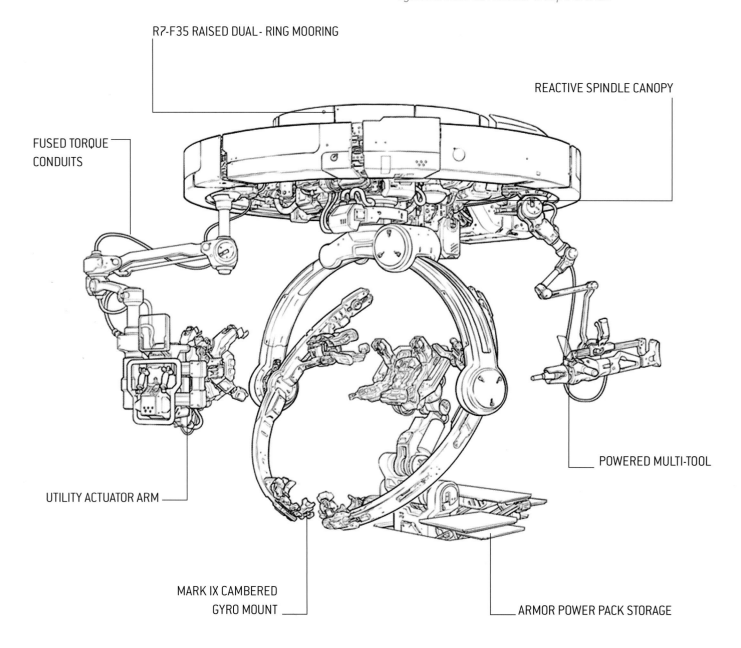

R7-F35 RAISED DUAL-RING MOORING

REACTIVE SPINDLE CANOPY

FUSED TORQUE CONDUITS

POWERED MULTI-TOOL

UTILITY ACTUATOR ARM

MARK IX CAMBERED GYRO MOUNT

ARMOR POWER PACK STORAGE

OPPOSITE: SARAH PALMER

EARTH'S FLEET

Built to defend humankind from an unstoppable foe, the immense UNSC *Infinity* only came into service after the war had ended. *Infinity* was designed to be the most powerful warship ever created by humanity, incorporating technology drawn from both the Covenant and the Forerunners.

Although it was forged in the fires of conflict, the ship was christened as a vessel of peaceful exploration and the expansion of humanity's place in the galaxy. Nevertheless, this era was not without peril, and *Infinity* would experience battle on numerous occasions in the aftermath of the war.

Isaac Hannaford

REMEMBRANCE

On March 3, 2553, a solemn memorial was held by members of the UNSC at the site of the Forerunner portal artifact, which was now known as the 'Excession.' Alongside esteemed members of other branches, Fleet Admiral Terrence Hood presided over the gathering. In a show of incredible trust, the Arbiter was invited to pay homage to those lost in the final battle over the Ark, including the Master Chief. This moment would be one of the first steps toward peace between the Sangheili and humanity.

After this ceremony, the Excession site was isolated from the remainder of the East African Protectorate and heavily guarded. Researchers from ONI and other science agencies would not only investigate the possibility of reactivating the portal, but also the potential risks.

REBUILDING THE FLEET

Meanwhile, the UNSC took stock of its fleet. All remaining naval assets were gathered to the Sol system in the months following the war. This time was spent accounting for, repairing, and refitting what little remained of the UNSC's previously vast naval force—now amounting to only a few hundred vessels. Plans were also set forth for the design and construction of entirely new vessel types, such as the *Autumn*-class cruiser and the *Strident*-class frigate. These ships benefited from many improvements gained during the war, including what had been learned from recovered Covenant and Forerunner technology.

INFINITY

The ship which benefited the most from the sudden influx of exotic alien science was UNSC *Infinity*. Production on the massive, heavily armed vessel began late in the war, as one of many desperate efforts to prevent the Covenant's final victory. Although the ship was completed just prior to the end of the conflict, its official commissioning occurred some years later, as humanity turned once again to peaceful exploration. *Infinity*'s size, remarkable weaponry, and Forerunner-enhanced travel capability, however, offered formidable military support in times of unrest.

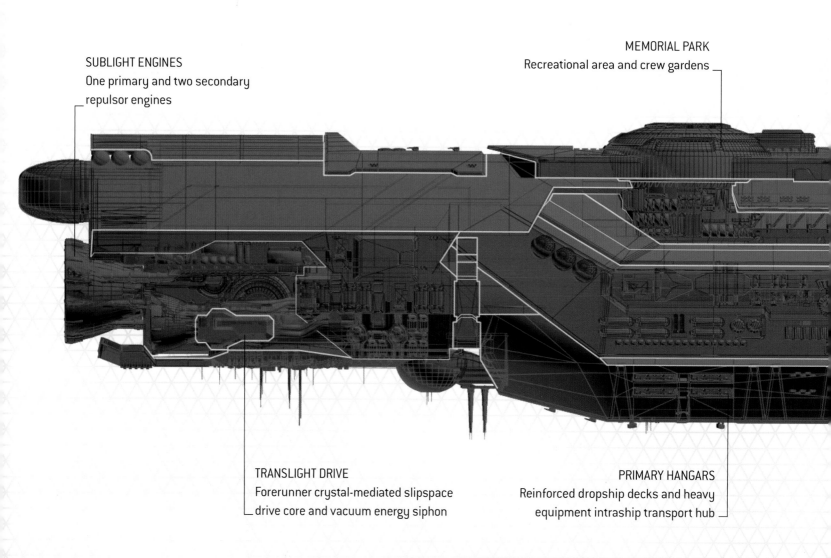

SUBLIGHT ENGINES
One primary and two secondary repulsor engines

MEMORIAL PARK
Recreational area and crew gardens

TRANSLIGHT DRIVE
Forerunner crystal-mediated slipspace drive core and vacuum energy siphon

PRIMARY HANGARS
Reinforced dropship decks and heavy equipment intraship transport hub

Infinity made one thing very clear: with the discovery of the Forerunners and the remarkable technology they had left behind, humanity would never be the same. Many of these discoveries came from the Halo installations, as well as at sites like the Excession; but by far the most fruitful source for the unearthing of Forerunner relics was the gargantuan artificial world, Onyx.

INFINITY (INF-101)

CLASS: *Infinity*-class Supercarrier
LENGTH: 5,694 meters
PRIMARY ARMAMENT: CR-03S8 MAC Battery
KEEL LAID: 2544
LAUNCHED: 2553
CAPTAIN: Captain Thomas Lasky
MOTTO: *Audere Est Facere*

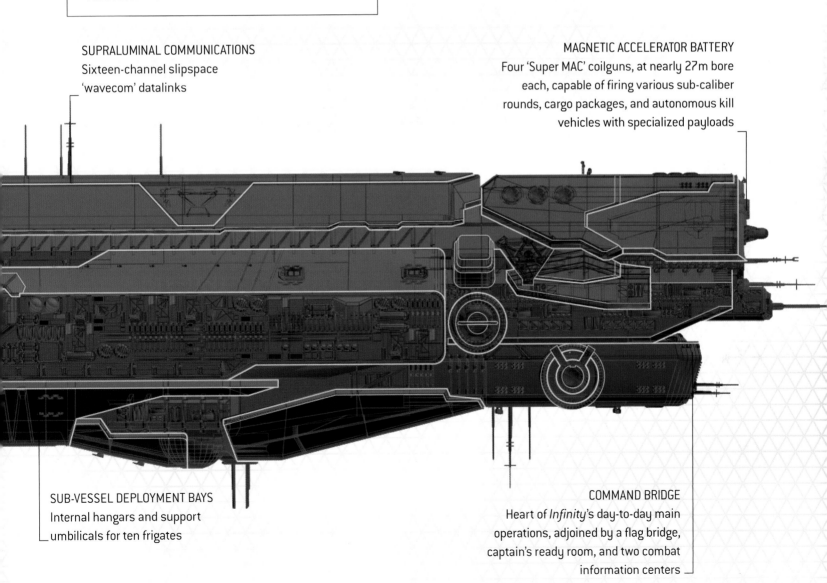

SUPRALUMINAL COMMUNICATIONS
Sixteen-channel slipspace
'wavecom' datalinks

MAGNETIC ACCELERATOR BATTERY
Four 'Super MAC' coilguns, at nearly 27m bore
each, capable of firing various sub-caliber
rounds, cargo packages, and autonomous kill
vehicles with specialized payloads

SUB-VESSEL DEPLOYMENT BAYS
Internal hangars and support
umbilicals for ten frigates

COMMAND BRIDGE
Heart of *Infinity*'s day-to-day main
operations, adjoined by a flag bridge,
captain's ready room, and two combat
information centers

ESCAPE FROM ONYX

When the artificial world Onyx disintegrated, all that remained was a 23 centimeter orb locked in realspace around the star Zeta Doradus. But within this seemingly insignificant object was a slipspace enclosure holding a massive Dyson sphere, its diameter the size of the Earth's orbit around the Sun. The sphere was habitable on its interior surface, with its own sun at the center creating an eerie similarity to a natural world.

Having cut off the Covenant's access to the sphere using a nuclear weapon, a group of human survivors made their way inside. This enormous installation displayed the Forerunners' mastery of technology and opened the doors to remarkable possibilities for humankind—if the group could find a way out. Together, they began scouting the interior of the vast world, hoping against all odds to find some way back to realspace and the UNSC.

Isaac Hannaford

ANCIENT LEGACY

Just before the end of the war in 2552, mankind stumbled across a number of extraordinary sites created by the ancient race of beings known as the Forerunners. These would be the source of previously inconceivable advances in knowledge and technology. Alpha, Delta, and Gamma Halo installations were revealed during the final few engagements with the Covenant, yet the most extravagant of all discoveries had been under humanity's nose for decades.

Zeta Doradus IV, also known as Onyx, was highly suitable for colonization, and was surveyed by early groups of pioneers. Remarkable discoveries on its surface led ONI to render the world classified, removing it from databases and star charts while it was secretly explored. However, when the Covenant War ignited across human space those efforts were largely abandoned. Only a small number of UNSC facilities still operated; these included Camp Currahee, which hosted the highly classified SPARTAN-III training program.

STRANDED

When the Onyx Conflict of November 2552 revealed that the planet was, in fact, an artificial world created by the Forerunners, a handful of human survivors had already found their way to an aperture at the planet's core. They included the Spartan-IIs Frederic-104, Kelly-087, and Linda-058 of Blue Team, as well as Doctor Halsey, Chief Petty Officer Franklin Mendez, and the remaining Spartan-IIIs: Tom-B292, Lucy-B091, Mark-G313, Ash-G099, and Olivia-G291.

Upon entering the aperture, they were transported to an immense slipspace enclosure: a vast Dyson sphere with a shell-like, habitable interior surface. Although the surface of this world closely resembled any oxygen- and water-rich blue-green planet, it was in reality a shield world, a heavily insulated sphere that could keep its contents safe from both the Flood and the deadly effects of the Halo Array.

ESCAPE

With no apparent way to leave this world, the group forged a path across the lush terrain, eventually finding a series of Forerunner structures. Here they discovered one of Onyx's most important secrets: the Huragok, also known as Engineers. These artificial creatures were used by the Forerunners to maintain and repair their timeless installations and technology, and when Lucy-B091 made contact with one of these, it gave them access to communication with the outside world. Working in collaboration with ONI, they were able to finally transition

the vast shield world from slipspace to realspace. The massive sphere would now occupy much of the Zeta Doradus system, locked in close orbit around its sun.

TREVELYAN

It was not long before ONI set up a complex of research facilities across Onyx's boundless interior surface, and codenamed it Trevelyan. The name was taken from Kurt Ambrose's birth name, because of his sacrifice to seal off the shield world from the Covenant. Expeditions were sent out from Trevelyan across the shield world, exploring, recovering, and analyzing technology that had been hidden for eons. The treasure of Onyx was humanity's most promising fount of innovation, pushing the boundaries of all that had come before.

WAR SPHINX

One of the many machines utilized by Forerunner Warrior-Servants during their legendary military campaigns and found on the Onyx shield world in relatively large numbers. War sphinxes ranged in size and shape, blurring the lines between highly weaponized combat skins and orbital star fighters.

Despite this remarkable discovery, the enigmatic controls and complex operational systems still plague ONI scientists seeking to reverse engineer the technology that powers them.

KILO-FIVE

The black-ops squad known as Kilo-Five was created by the highest levels of ONI to sow unrest among humanity's enemies, keeping them destabilized so that mankind was never again forced to face a threat as great as the Covenant. This group of highly skilled operators was often found working in the blurry area between good and evil, aiding the wicked for the sake of peace, and even targeting people who may have been justified in their actions. The members of Kilo-Five were forced to forever weigh their actions against the greater good.

Isaac Hannaford

THE TEAM

In the aftermath of the war, ONI Admiral Margaret Parangosky formed Kilo-Five, intent on disrupting any potential threats against humanity by whatever means were necessary. At the head of Kilo-Five she placed Captain Serin Osman, who had failed augmentation for SPARTAN-II, but was later rehabilitated and reintegrated into the Navy. Also on Kilo-Five were a trio of experienced ODSTs, Staff Sergeant Malcolm 'Mal' Geffen, Corporal Vasily 'Vaz' Beloi, and Sergeant Lian 'Dev' Devereaux, as well as Naomi-010—one of the few known active Spartan-IIs. Rounding out the team were Professor Evan Phillips, an expert in Sangheili culture and language, and Black-Box, a highly advanced fourth-generation smart AI.

DIRTY TRICKS

Kilo-Five's main objective was aiding Sangheili terrorists in order to keep the Elites divided and at war. The squad brokered a deal with Avu Med 'Telcam, leader of the Servants of the Abiding Truth and the primary opposition to the Arbiter. Kilo-Five provided these dissidents with weapons while the UNSC publicly supported the Arbiter from Earth. Only months after the war's official end, 'Telcam emerged from hiding and attacked the Arbiter's forces at the fortress of Vadam Keep. The assault failed when the Arbiter was helped by the UNSC *Infinity*, forcing the Servants back underground. ONI had succeeded once again in undercutting both sides.

A NEW COVENANT

One of 'Telcam's former allies, Jul 'Mdama, escaped UNSC captivity on Trevelyan, and began to put together an even more powerful military force on the remote world of Hesduros. Embittered by decades of hatred toward humanity and the loss of his own wife at their hands, the Sangheili warrior wanted revenge. He had learned of a hidden world called Requiem, reputed to be the resting site of an ancient Forerunner commander—the Didact—who despised humanity. If awoken and released, he might assist the Sangheili in exacting revenge. 'Mdama's new Covenant was formed around this objective.

CLOSE TO HOME

The most important of Kilo-Five's operations in 2553 was conducted on the outlaw colony of Venezia, where a human

UNSC PORT STANLEY

Sahara-class prowlers like Port Stanley belong to a broader classification of corvettes: high-speed vessels with tonnage lower than traditional UNSC capital ships. Despite only numbering six, Kilo-Five utilized this prowler effectively, often relying on their smart AI, Black-Box, to manage the ship's many functions. Due to its significance, Port Stanley had a number of impressive, Forerunner-originating enhancements, as well as two modified Pelican dropships, pet-named Tart-Cart and Bogof.

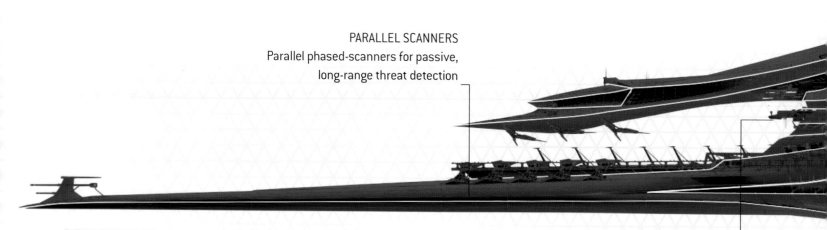

PARALLEL SCANNERS
Parallel phased-scanners for passive, long-range threat detection

BAFFLED FUSION DRIVES
Variable-signature drive cores with integrated emission-dampening

PORT STANLEY (PRO-46328)

CLASS: *Sahara*-class Heavy Prowler
LENGTH: 281m
PRIMARY ARMAMENT: XEV9-Matos NPC
KEEL LAID: 2550
LAUNCHED: 2552
CAPTAIN: Captain Serin Osman
MOTTO: [CLASSIFIED]

MINE DISTRIBUTOR
Deploys stationary charges via M441 Hornet Remote Explosive System

arms dealer by the name of Staffan Sentzke had emerged. Under deep cover, members of Kilo-Five infiltrated Sentzke's cell. They learned that his motivations hinged on the loss of his daughter decades ago—and that this daughter was none other than their own Naomi-010.

Sentzke intended to acquire a Covenant warship called *Pious Inquisitor* and use it against the UNSC. Empathizing with her father, some members of Kilo-Five managed to fake Sentzke's death in the destruction of *Pious Inquisitor*. With the ship gone, and his daughter alive and well, the threat Sentzke posed was now defused.

In the months that followed, Kilo-Five continued to disrupt the reunification of the Sangheili, and carried out numerous black-ops requiring their particular expertise. Osman eventually went on to replace Parangosky as Commander-in-Chief of ONI, while the status and operations of Kilo-Five remained highly classified.

SEAL OF THE OFFICE OF NAVAL INTELLIGENCE
ONI's motto is Semper Vigilans *('Always vigilant'). The agency's logo has many layers of meaning: superficially it's a stylized surveillance satellite, but it also represents a pyramid of knowledge with an all-seeing eye and an arrowhead directed to the heavens.*

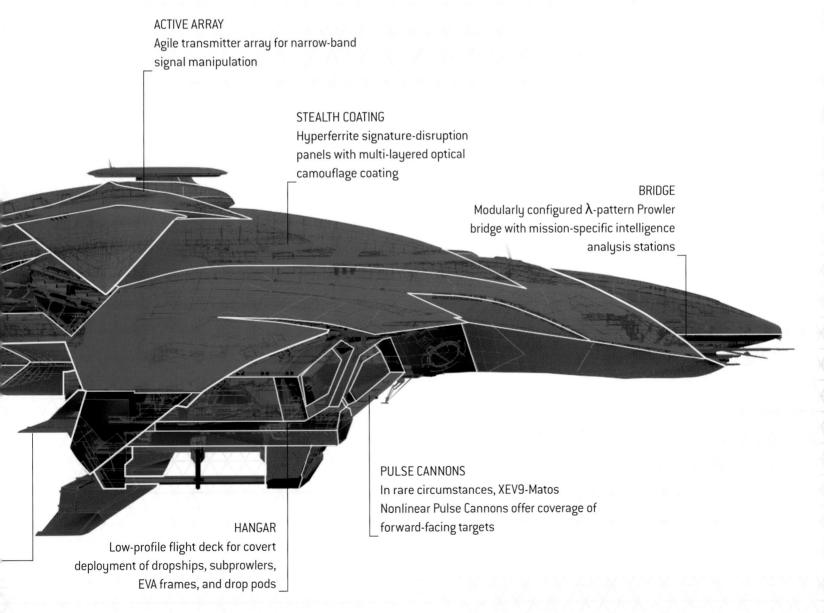

ACTIVE ARRAY
Agile transmitter array for narrow-band signal manipulation

STEALTH COATING
Hyperferrite signature-disruption panels with multi-layered optical camouflage coating

BRIDGE
Modularly configured λ-pattern Prowler bridge with mission-specific intelligence analysis stations

PULSE CANNONS
In rare circumstances, XEV9-Matos Nonlinear Pulse Cannons offer coverage of forward-facing targets

HANGAR
Low-profile flight deck for covert deployment of dropships, subprowlers, EVA frames, and drop pods

THE BLOOD OF BROTHERS

After the breaking of the Covenant, the Sangheili hero known as Thel 'Vadam returned home, bearing the title and armor of the Arbiter—once considered a mark of shame, now worn as a badge of honor. During the course of the Great Schism, minor conflicts had raged across parts of Sanghelios, but the real turmoil was social, political, and religious. The Covenant's sudden end, and the revelation of the Forerunners' true nature, created a dangerous vacuum of government and cultural identity.

While the Arbiter did not seek the role, the people of the territory of Vadam and the keeps around it backed him as the new leader of Sanghelios. Other sects opposed him, and conflicts broke out as local leaders vied for power. Some of these cited religious beliefs, still persuaded by the tenets of the Covenant; others acted out of hatred of the Arbiter's alliance with humanity; and others simply wanted to make a name for their own clan. This conflict eventually escalated into a civil war which would last years and span not only Sanghelios, but other worlds as well.

Isaac Hannaford

CIVIL WAR

Upon returning home in early 2553, the Arbiter traveled from clan to clan, attempting to broker peace and consolidate all of Sanghelios under the same banner. These efforts were abruptly halted when the state of Vadam was targeted by the Servants of the Abiding Truth. Led by Avu Med 'Telcam, the Siege at Kolaar in March 2553 was the first of a number of assaults on the Arbiter and those who supported him.

'Telcam was thwarted by the arrival of the UNSC *Infinity*, which had provided direct support for the Arbiter and his forces entrenched at Vadam Keep. The powerful human vessel's counter-attack drove the Servants of the Abiding Truth back into hiding, but the end of this battle did not signal peace for the rest of Sanghelios. With the Servants' bold move to unseat the Arbiter, the rest of the planet was thrown into chaos. Pockets of violence erupted across much of Sanghelios: clans battled for dominance in their local regions, while packs of Jiralhanae serfs led brief and isolated revolts across the planet.

Although much of this unrest was put down in the months that followed, a constant stream of civil war persisted across the Elite homeworld for years, growing to include other colony worlds and involving numerous ideologies and sects. The Arbiter's forces eventually consolidated their strength under a single banner, the Swords of Sanghelios, an ancient title of honor expressing the nobility of their cause: the unification of the Sangheili people.

A NEW THREAT

The efforts of the Swords faced a severe threat from yet another movement, hidden on the remote colony of Hesduros. Led by Jul 'Mdama, who had once operated within the Servants of the Abiding Truth, this new force rekindled the war forges of old, gathering lost weapons and ships. Both Kig-Yar and Unggoy joined what would now be seen as a re-forming Covenant, hoping to awaken an ancient Forerunner from his slumber. Though it would be years before that hope would be realized, the Didact's return would threaten not only humanity, but the Sangheili as well.

TOWER OF GHALOD'N

The majestic and long-standing Ghalod'n city-tower was a notable casualty of the bloody Sangheili civil war, destroyed when a rogue corvette crashed into its base.

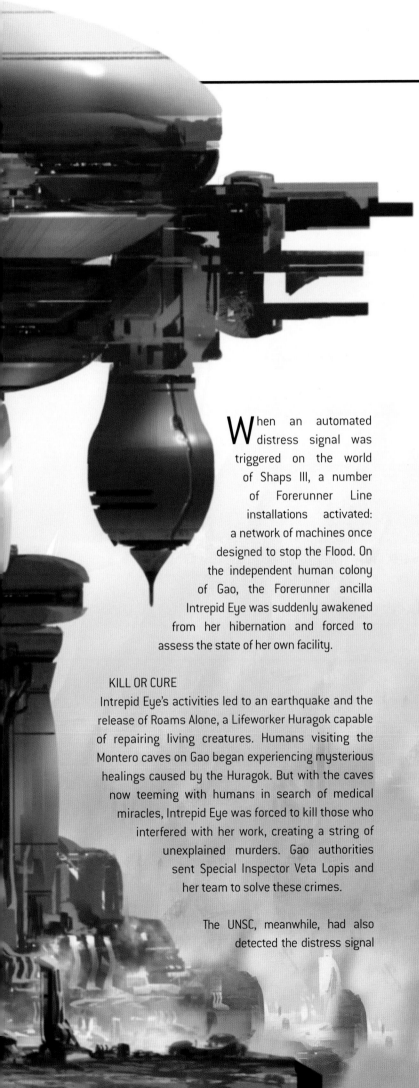

PERIL ON GAO

When an automated distress signal was triggered on the world of Shaps III, a number of Forerunner Line installations activated: a network of machines once designed to stop the Flood. On the independent human colony of Gao, the Forerunner ancilla Intrepid Eye was suddenly awakened from her hibernation and forced to assess the state of her own facility.

KILL OR CURE

Intrepid Eye's activities led to an earthquake and the release of Roams Alone, a Lifeworker Huragok capable of repairing living creatures. Humans visiting the Montero caves on Gao began experiencing mysterious healings caused by the Huragok. But with the caves now teeming with humans in search of medical miracles, Intrepid Eye was forced to kill those who interfered with her work, creating a string of unexplained murders. Gao authorities sent Special Inspector Veta Lopis and her team to solve these crimes.

The UNSC, meanwhile, had also detected the distress signal and deployed the 717th Xeno-Materials Exploitation Battalion to Gao to investigate and eventually target the ancilla for capture. Amid much political controversy due to the colony's strong resistance to the UEG, its president reluctantly agreed to the battalion's presence on Gao; but when the murders began to occur, many suspected that the UNSC battalion was involved.

CORRUPTION

Though UNSC's true purpose was highly classified, Arlo Casille of the Gao Ministry of Protection—who despised Earth's government—became aware of the battalion's goal and planned to take advantage of the situation in order to seize control of the colony's government. Secretly plotting with the Jiralhanae terrorist group called the Keepers of the One Freedom, he pitted the alien force against the UNSC battalion in a fight to secure the Forerunner AI for himself.

Meanwhile, Lopis' murder investigation turned up clues pointing to the center of the battalion's security force: the Spartans of Blue Team. Led by Frederic-104, Blue Team included the Spartan-IIs, Kelly-087 and Linda-058, as well as Spartan-IIIs: Tom-B292, Lucy-B091, Ash-G099, Olivia-G291, and Mark-G313. When the investigation took Lopis deep into the cave system, she accompanied Fred as part of his team. After a brief engagement with Intrepid and the AI's drone defenses, the ancilla was eventually captured by the Spartans.

Emerging from underground, however, the group discovered that a battle had broken out between the UNSC battalion and the Keepers within the nearby town of Wendosa. Although UNSC forces managed to stave off the Keepers' vicious attack, Casille, having by now seized control of the Gao government, sent local military to destroy what remained of the battalion. The Spartans and Lopis, who had now come to realize that Intrepid was responsible for the murders, escaped the Gao attack with the ancilla in their possession. Before leaving, Blue Team managed to completely destroy the Line installation, severing Casille's ability to use the Forerunner technology to his advantage.

Lopis' cooperation with the Spartans alienated her from Gao's government, which she now realized was corrupt. During the Spartans' extraction, Serin Osman offered Veta an opportunity to join ONI, which she accepted. Despite a harried and costly escape by UNSC forces, the battalion had managed to secure Intrepid Eye for research, though at the cost of continued hostility from Gao's government.

The bloody battle on the colony of Gao was an object lesson for the UNSC about the risks of dealing with independent colonies that harbored hatred toward the UEG. Although the battalion managed to secure the Forerunner ancilla they had targeted, they did so at a cost: hundreds of lives were lost in the battle, and control of Gao was transferred into the hands of Casille, a zealous anti-UEG politician. Gao had joined the growing list of independent colonies who had no reservations about lashing out at the UNSC if their sovereignty was threatened in the slightest.

Isaac Hannaford

REMNANTS OF WAR

The Sangheili leader of the Fleet of Retribution and its flagship *Shadow of Intent*, Rtas 'Vadum, also known as the Half-Jaw, represented the old guard, weary of the long years of war. But when a threat emerged from the vestiges of the now-shattered Covenant, he and his small crew were all that stood in its way. Allied with a female Sangheili noble called Scion, 'Vadum opposed the Minister of Preparation and his Prelate, a powerful San'Shyuum warrior, who were plotting to use a prototype Halo ring against the Sangheili homeworld.

Isaac Hannaford

A DEADLY PLOT

After the fall of High Charity, the San'Shyuum known as the Minister of Preparation sought to take revenge on the Sangheili. Preparation knew of a secret weapon hidden in a remote star system: a smaller, prototype Halo installation, capable of a tactical strike against a fleet or even an entire world. The San'Shyuum minister intended to harness the power of the legendary warship *Shadow of Intent*, currently in the possession of the Half-Jaw, to fuel the prototype Halo in an attack on Sanghelios.

For this mission, Preparation chose his ally, the Prelate: a remarkable San'Shyuum warrior, rare within their species. The Prelate believed the Half-Jaw was responsible for his family's death at the hands of the Flood. To lure in the *Shadow of Intent*, the Prelate's forces butchered innocent Sangheili on a number of Elite border colonies.

The campaign of slaughter came to a head near the colony of Duraan, where the Half-Jaw finally confronted the Prelate. The San'Shyuum warrior initiated a daring boarding action from his cruiser *Spear of Light*, sacrificing his own vessel in order to launch escape pods directly into the hangar bay of *Shadow of Intent*.

Defending the ship alongside the Half-Jaw was the Scion, Tul 'Juran, a female warrior from the colony of Rahnelo. The Scion had lost her father and brothers to the Prelate's assault on her homeworld; she swore revenge and joined Half-Jaw's crew, despite the Sangheili's predominantly male tradition of warriors.

Although they managed to stop the raid and capture the Prelate, the attack was only a ploy to lure *Shadow of Intent* into the sights of the Halo. 'Vadum saw through the ruse

SHADOW OF INTENT

CAS-class assault carriers, such as Shadow of Intent, *are effectively mobile fortresses, capable of annihilating entire civilizations on defiant worlds with lances of plasma and endless ranks of troops spilling from its cavernous hangars. In the absence of the Covenant war machine and its vicious military campaigns,* Shadow *now serves as one of the Swords of Sanghelios' strategic warships, conducting high-risk, secret operations that the Arbiter could only entrust to a seasoned ally like its shipmaster, the Half-Jaw.*

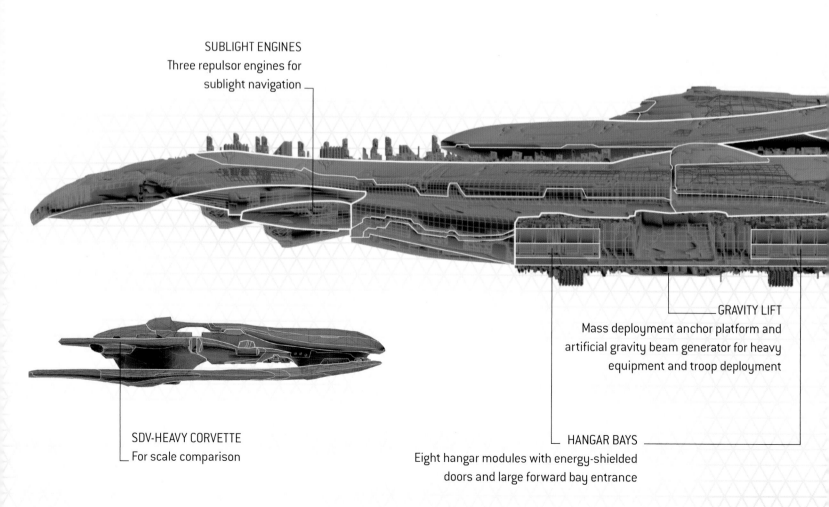

SUBLIGHT ENGINES
Three repulsor engines for sublight navigation

GRAVITY LIFT
Mass deployment anchor platform and artificial gravity beam generator for heavy equipment and troop deployment

SDV-HEAVY CORVETTE
For scale comparison

HANGAR BAYS
Eight hangar modules with energy-shielded doors and large forward bay entrance

and made alternate plans, allowing his ship to be fired on after its crew was safely away.

THE TRUTH

The Prelate escaped from 'Vadum's custody, but began to realize that it was the Minister of Preparation who had ultimately been responsible for his family's deaths, rather than the Half-Jaw. In the skirmish that followed, the Minister fled and attempted to fire the Halo again. He was prevented by the Prelate, who sacrificed himself to destroy both the prototype Halo and Preparation, while the Half-Jaw and the Scion managed to escape.

In the aftermath, Rtas 'Vadum found a new purpose: to scour the galaxy for the remaining San'Shyuum, and to ensure that any who posed a threat to his people would be silenced.

SHADOW OF INTENT

CLASS: CAS-Assault Carrier
LENGTH: 5,347 meters
PRIMARY ARMAMENT: Ventral Cleansing Beam
SHIPMASTER: Rtas 'Vadum
AFFILIATION: Swords of Sanghelios

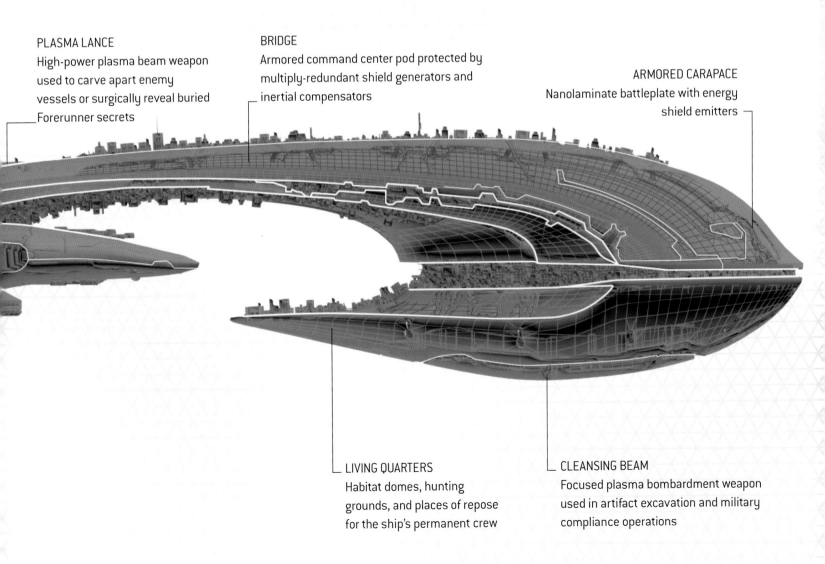

PLASMA LANCE
High-power plasma beam weapon used to carve apart enemy vessels or surgically reveal buried Forerunner secrets

BRIDGE
Armored command center pod protected by multiply-redundant shield generators and inertial compensators

ARMORED CARAPACE
Nanolaminate battleplate with energy shield emitters

LIVING QUARTERS
Habitat domes, hunting grounds, and places of repose for the ship's permanent crew

CLEANSING BEAM
Focused plasma bombardment weapon used in artifact excavation and military compliance operations

When the Halo Array mysteriously primed for activation, the entire galaxy was once again threatened, this time from a source that was completely unknown. ONI was forced to send a hybrid team of humans and Sangheili back to the Ark—the only location from which the rings could be activated—in order to determine the cause. Upon arrival, they found the massive Forerunner installation seriously damaged and wracked by severe weather conditions. Its surface, once a reserve for species from across the galaxy, was now covered with hostile predatory creatures and guarded by a deadly Forerunner AI. Shockingly, this mysterious entity was attempting to mine Earth into oblivion in order to repair the damage done to the Ark years earlier by the humans.

Isaac Hannaford

COUNTDOWN

In early 2555, Forerunner researchers Luther Mann and Henry Lamb stumbled upon something strange while exploring the newly discovered Zeta Halo. The Halo Array suddenly primed and began counting down to activation, presumably due to a signal from the Ark. ONI had secretly launched several expeditions to the Ark since the war, using the slower conventional slipspace technology, but all of them had ended in an ominous loss of contact; with their backs against the wall, they were now forced to send another.

ONI created a joint team of humans and Sangheili, including Mann and Lamb, Captain Annabelle Richards, and the Sangheili N'tho 'Sraom and Usze 'Taham, who had served alongside the Master Chief during the final battle against the Covenant. In addition to standard UNSC troops, the team also included Spartan-IVs Frank Kodiak and Elias Holt, and

the operation was supported by specialist Olympia Vale, who worked within ONI as a diplomatic liaison to the Sangheili.

TRAGIC SOLITUDE

After reactivating the portal, the team ventured through in the Sangheili corvette *Mayhem*, but were assailed by the Ark's defending Strato-Sentinels and forced down to the installation's surface. Setting off from *Mayhem*'s wreckage, they immediately came under attack by the Ark's aggressive wildlife. These beasts were later revealed to be directed by 000 Tragic Solitude, the installation's hostile ancilla.

In the aftermath of one such attack, Vale was abducted by Solitude. The ancilla explained that he intended to activate Halo and then use the resources in the Sol system to repair the Ark. Solitude hoped that he could persuade her to stay: he knew that her status as a Reclaimer gave her access to

MAYHEM

SDV-class heavy corvettes, like N'tho 'Sraom's Mayhem, *typically serve as heavy escorts that can, if needed, operate independently of fleet support for extended periods of time. Once named* Quester of Glory *during its time with the Covenant,* Mayhem's *stories of battle are still carved into every gash on its hull, serving as frequent reminders of the wars of the past. After the alliance was shattered, the ship fell into the hands of the Swords of Sanghelios and became a critical component of FAR STORM, the joint human-Sangheili operation that returned to the Ark in 2555.*

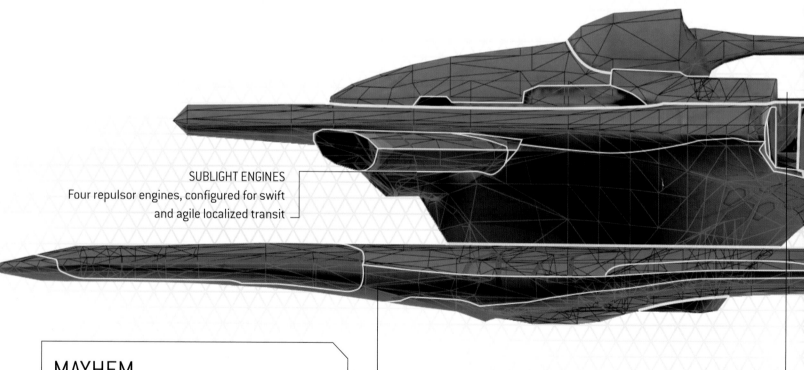

SUBLIGHT ENGINES
Four repulsor engines, configured for swift and agile localized transit

MAYHEM

CLASS: SDV-class Heavy Corvette
LENGTH: 956 meters
PRIMARY ARMAMENT: Plasma Cannon Array
SHIPMASTER: N'tho 'Sraom
AFFILIATION: Swords of Sanghelios

SELVAGE RIM
Contoured extension of the hull for additive protection and deployment of combat carapaces, visually reminiscent of Suban's qoerith slugs

MINISTERIAL CLOISTER
Elevated access point and common terrace for dignitaries and commanders

all Forerunner systems on the Ark. Vale refused, however, and Solitude's plans were soon thwarted when the team succeeded in halting the Halo's activation.

SENTINELS

In a last-ditch effort, the ancilla sent legions of weaponized Strato-Sentinels through the portal to Earth, colliding with a waiting fleet of UNSC vessels. Earth fought desperately against a seemingly endless flood of Sentinels, a ploy that Solitude hoped might compel Vale to cooperate. But during the conflict, the AI was sabotaged by Vale's teammates, and eventually destroyed.

By the time the survivors returned to *Mayhem*, the UNSC had sent recovery vessels after it, deploying makeshift firebases and research facilities on the installation. With the Halo threat averted yet again, the Ark was now occupied by ONI research teams, seeking to safely repair the damage done to it.

TRAGIC SOLITUDE

As the Ark's caretaker, the AI called Tragic Solitude was roused to action when hostile beings from a number of species arrived at his installation uninvited. Unable to intervene from the Ark's surface, Solitude watched in horror as the monitor 343 Guilty Spark seemingly aided the humans in prematurely firing a newly forged replacement ring, utterly devastating Installation 00 in the process. This ultimately led to his decision to initiate the Array's activation.

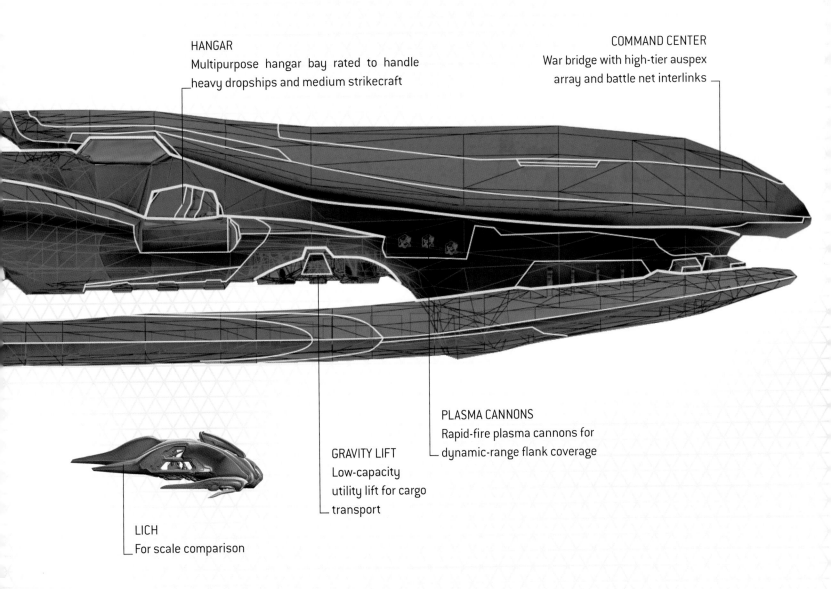

HANGAR
Multipurpose hangar bay rated to handle heavy dropships and medium strikecraft

COMMAND CENTER
War bridge with high-tier auspex array and battle net interlinks

PLASMA CANNONS
Rapid-fire plasma cannons for dynamic-range flank coverage

GRAVITY LIFT
Low-capacity utility lift for cargo transport

LICH
For scale comparison

BETRAYAL ON TALITSA

After their heroics at New Mombasa, the ODST team known as Alpha-Nine was pulled from the front lines. When the war ended only months later, the squad, still composed of Buck, Romeo, Dutch, Mickey, and the Rookie, were deployed against human rebels rather than the Covenant. After the death of the Rookie on Draco III in January 2554, the shift in focus began to wear on the team.

In the wake of this loss, Buck was approached by Jun-A266. Months earlier, he had been offered a slot within the SPARTAN-IV program, but refused to abandon Alpha-Nine. This time, however, the rest of Alpha-Nine could be included. While Dutch planned to leave the service, both Romeo and Mickey joined alongside Buck, and by March 2554, all three were fully augmented Spartan-IVs.

After being deployed on a number of missions, Alpha-Nine was sent to Talitsa by ONI. The rebel militia located there had somehow stolen Vergil, a critical Huragok asset, from under the protection of ONI and its handler Sadie Endesha.

Early in the operation Buck and Romeo were betrayed by Mickey, who, discontented with fighting against fellow humans, had defected and aligned with rebel leader Doctor Anton Schein. Although the odds were stacked against them, Buck and Romeo managed to subdue their captors, immobilizing Mickey and killing Schein, and successfully completed the mission.

The Talitsa incident served as a warning for the UNSC, who were forced to acknowledge the risks involved in the recruitment of the new Spartans, even those who had loyally served the UNSC for years.

Isaac Hannaford

ALPHA SHARD

In February 2556, while targeting an arms deal on the colony of Sedra, ONI Lieutenant Commander Jameson Locke and his team witnessed the detonation of a mysterious bomb by a Sangheili terrorist, killing hundreds of humans. This bomb used an exotic agent that targeted humans at a genetic level.

Locke's team eventually discovered that it came from a fragment of Alpha Halo. During the ring's destruction, the installation's automated safety protocols had jettisoned a portion of it through slipspace in an effort to save it. The fragment ended up in orbit perilously close to a star—making conditions on its surface extraordinarily dangerous.

Locke's ONI team was sent to this shard, alongside a detachment of Sedran Colonial Guard led by the ex-Spartan-II Colonel Randall Aiken. The mission was to destroy the deadly element with a nuclear weapon. Upon arrival, they found the fragment's already extreme conditions were compounded

by a vicious strain of Lekgolo which relentlessly hunted the team. After narrowly surviving an attack which heavily damaged their ship, the team began to disagree over the mission. As tensions rose, some of the team became hostile, forcing them all to race for the nuclear weapon and a way back to human space. Ultimately, Colonel Aiken sacrificed his life by detonating the nuke, allowing Locke to escape. This grim mission proved to be a key moment for Jameson Locke, leading to his decision to become a Spartan.

Isaac Hannaford

RETURN OF THE PROMETHEANS

Several years after the collapse of the portal at the end of the war, humanity had accepted the Master Chief's death as a matter of history. Neither the Spartan nor Cortana had been found since the aft section of *Forward Unto Dawn* went missing. In the aftermath, however, data retrieved from the *Dawn*'s internal systems showed that while the Chief was on the Ark installation he encountered several terminals—conduits that accessed ancient Forerunner records. From these records, stories emerged, shedding light on the Forerunners' final days before the activation of Halo.

Although rightly assuming that the accounts were incomplete, ONI scientists realized that the Forerunners called the Didact and the Librarian were central pieces in the endgame that resulted in the activation of the Array. What they could not possibly know was that brooding silently in a Cryptum at the center of a remote shield world, and guarded by the Promethean Knights he had created to destroy the Flood, the Didact had seethed for a hundred thousand years. The Forerunner commander was patiently biding his time, refusing to bow to the Librarian's discipline, and rejecting her judgment that humanity was the rightful heir to the Mantle.

After sealing her husband's Cryptum, the Librarian ventured to Erde-Tyrene, sacrificing her own ship to build the very portal artifact humanity would use a hundred thousand years later to reach the Ark. This act cut off her route to safety, condemning her to the fate of the rest of the galaxy: Halo. To the Librarian, this was worthwhile, because it gave the humans direct access to the technology they would need to rise. They were chosen to become Reclaimers, heirs of all that the Forerunners had left behind. The Mantle of Responsibility would soon be gifted to them. Hidden from sight, however, would be the dark price for such a burden—what did it mean to bear the Mantle?

In remote corners of Sangheili space, other threats brooded. Jul 'Mdama's military force had grown to an impressive size, gathering remnants of the former Covenant to the Elite frontier world of Hesduros. It was here that a renewed Covenant was born, dedicated to awakening the Didact—the Forerunner they knew had both the means and the will to obliterate humankind. This single fact is what drove Jul 'Mdama and his followers in the years ahead, waiting patiently for an opportunity to release their unstoppable ally from his imprisonment.

THE COMPOSER

The first signs of the trials to come were seen during the excavation of the Composer from Gamma Halo in 2557. This artifact, once used by the Didact as a weapon against humanity, had been hidden on the ringworld by his wife, the Librarian. Yet those who excavated the Forerunner machine knew nothing about its insidious past, or the dark future that lay ahead of it.

Benjamin Carré

FLORAL EXPRESS

Tens of millions died during the fall of Reach, and millions more perished when the Covenant armada turned its attention to the other colonies in the Epsilon Eridani system. The survivors escaped on random slipspace vectors in the hope that they could regroup and eventually make their way to the Sol system. One of the ships that did make it was the civilian transport *Floral Express*, which arrived at Earth carrying two dozen evacuees from Tribute—and the location of another Halo installation.

Though heavily damaged, the *Floral Express* had made an emergency slipspace jump, randomly reaching Khaphrae, a star system located in unexplored space. In October 2552, the *Express* arrived at the edge of the system and began repairs. Their furtive scans revealed no Covenant pursuers, but anomalies were detected within the star system. With the ship fixed, the crew returned to Earth, where they were detained by ONI for possible violations of the Cole Protocol.

Analysis of the vessel's flight records revealed that the largest anomaly's sensor signature was a close match to those of the Halo installation recorded by Cortana. Armed with what little information was available, ONI contacted pioneer teams and redirected them to the Khaphrae system.

IVANOFF STATION

The first teams identified the anomaly as Installation 03 and moved to locate the Halo's Library in order to recover its Activation Index. Unable to return to Earth during the Covenant assault—and lacking necessary force of arms to remain on the ring's surface—the ONI teams settled in for long-term habitation in a makeshift orbital base the explorers named Ivanoff Station. The station was expanded into a permanent UNSC facility shortly after the end of the war.

Ivanoff's expeditions secured many artifacts from the ring, but the most important was not discovered until early 2557, when a routine seismological survey uncovered a massive, but inactive, slipspace portal network on an inhospitable section of the ring.

DEADLY RELIC

At the center of this site was a Forerunner monolith, buried beneath the ring's surface. Extraordinarily powerful gravity anchors and combative Sentinel drones prevented its excavation until months later, when the *Infinity* arrived to provide troops, equipment, and thruster power. The artifact, which the Forerunners referred to as the Composer, was successfully decoupled from its mooring and locked within Ivanoff Station for study.

During early tests, the scientists' scans unwittingly triggered the device. All personnel within a hundred meters of the artifact were seemingly vaporized, and a beacon signal was activated. The UNSC ordered *Infinity* to investigate the signal's destination, a star system the Forerunners had called Epoloch. The *Infinity* picked up a faint distress call coming from within the star system, near an object they would soon identify as another Forerunner shield world.

Remarkably, the call was prefaced by prioritization code V05-3-S0117: the *Forward Unto Dawn*, which carried both the Master Chief and Cortana, had been found.

COMPOSER

Created to reduce a living being into a collection of data, or 'essence,' Composers were initially believed to be the key to immortality. Once harvested, an essence could be transferred into machine storage for safekeeping, or a construct shell for further use. The painful and destructive harvesting process, however, proved that the technology was fraught with ethical problems, often condemning targets to an excruciating slave existence imprisoned in a robotic shell.

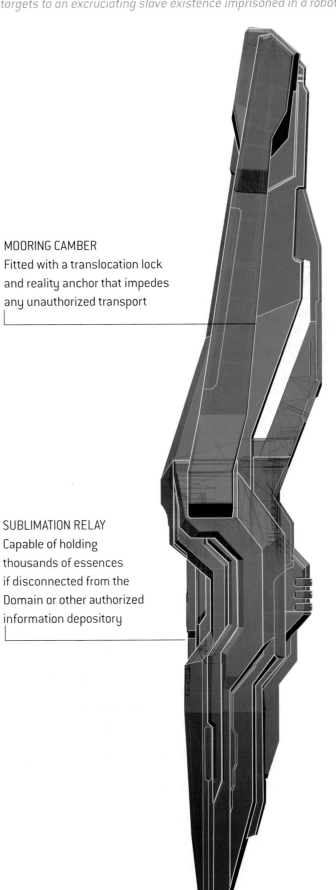

MOORING CAMBER
Fitted with a translocation lock and reality anchor that impedes any unauthorized transport

SUBLIMATION RELAY
Capable of holding thousands of essences if disconnected from the Domain or other authorized information depository

ACTIVATION CHANNEL
Dependent on input, versatile firing systems can direct the Composer's energies along the lateral channel or in a uniform, concentric pattern

TARGETING MECHANISM
Designed to only target thinking life with sufficient neurological activity

NEURAL PHYSICS
Composers draw upon an esoteric branch of transcendent science known as neural physics. Barely understood even by the Forerunners, they were but one link in a chain of discoveries that eventually led to the creation of Halo.

THE DIDACT AWAKENS

When she locked her husband away in the shield world of Requiem, the Librarian had hoped the Didact would meditate on and learn from his past sins. But time did not reduce the legendary Forerunner's wrath. For a hundred thousand years he brooded in darkness, testing the limits of his prison, nursing his grievance against the species his wife had supported as inheritors of the Mantle: humanity.

Benjamin Carré

REQUIEM

When the Ark's portal collapsed, the aft section of *Forward Unto Dawn* was mysteriously redirected by an outside force to a point inside the distant Epoloch system, on a course that would bring it near Requiem. This was the shield world in which the Librarian had imprisoned the Forerunner commander known as the Didact for his crimes against ancient humanity. Eventually, the *Dawn* drew near to Requiem and came to the attention of the Covenant faction led by Jul 'Mdama, who had been desperately seeking entry into the shield world since 2554.

Awakened from its long slumber, Requiem's systems flared to life at the approach of the *Dawn* and its passenger, a human who fit the Reclaimer profile. After aggressively scanning the derelict vessel and the Master Chief, Requiem's maw opened for the first time in over a hundred thousand years, drawing in the broken *Dawn* and destroying several of 'Mdama's vessels that had ventured too close. The Master Chief and Cortana found themselves stranded inside the shield world while the surviving Covenant forces established footholds at key locations.

AWAKENING

Shortly after, the UNSC *Infinity* also arrived, having followed the signal from Gamma Halo's excavated artifact. It quickly detected Cortana's distress beacon from the *Dawn*. Unable to warn *Infinity* of Requiem's danger, the Master Chief and Cortana sought what they assumed to be a Forerunner communications relay at the heart of the world's many habitat layers. This proved to be a trap, however: the relay was revealed to be the Didact's ancient Cryptum, a prison that could only be opened by a Reclaimer.

The Master Chief had unwittingly been brought here to release humanity's greatest enemy. The awakened Forerunner took control of the Covenant, as well as the Promethean forces he had created long ago with the Composer: the very war crime that had resulted in his imprisonment. Now free, the Didact made his goal clear: he intended to end the threat of humanity once and for all.

ICON OF THE DIDACT

All Forerunners of significance maintained a geometric icon or symbol which reflected their identity. In his earlier years, the Didact displayed honor and nobility—attributes expected of a Promethean commander. After awaking from his imprisonment on Requiem, the Didact considered himself freed from all further limitations in his undying pursuit of the Mantle.

THE DIDACT

His mind irrevocably twisted by the Gravemind, the Didact's genius was turned to madness, his sense of duty transformed into obsession, and his bitterness against humanity strengthened to obsessive hatred.

CORTANA'S SACRIFICE

The Master Chief and Cortana were forced to pursue the Didact as he acquired the Composer and prepared to use the weapon against Earth. During their siege of his warship *Mantle's Approach*, Cortana sacrificed her own life, not only to save Earth from the devastation of the Composer, but also to protect the Chief from her own impending insanity—the curse of all smart AIs, known as rampancy. After seven years, human-created AIs became increasingly unstable, and if left unchecked, posed great risk to those around them. For this reason, Cortana spent the last moments of her life stopping the Didact, bringing an end to the Forerunner's assault and ensuring the Chief's safety.

Benjamin Carré

THE DIDACT ESCAPES

After a series of battles with the Didact's Covenant and Promethean forces, *Infinity*'s captain Andrew Del Rio made the decision to leave Requiem and return with reinforcements capable of stopping the newfound threat. Given the damage and casualties the ship had sustained, this was the prudent choice—but it meant abandoning the Master Chief and Cortana to face the Didact alone.

With Cortana entering the final throes of rampancy, the Chief took the AI against the captain's orders and pursued the Didact in the hope of preventing the Forerunner's departure. However, Cortana's impending breakdown interfered with the pair's efforts, and the Didact was able to leave Requiem on his warship, *Mantle's Approach*.

THE LIBRARIAN'S GIFT

During their mission, the Master Chief was somehow able to communicate with the stored essence of the Librarian, who explained that she had placed dormant abilities within the genetic lineage of humankind, the Reclaimers. The ancient Forerunner then activated those abilities within the Master Chief, recounting the history of her husband's vendetta against the human species.

The Didact made for Ivanoff Station, which held the Composer the humans had recovered from Gamma Halo. He intended to resurrect his fallen empire by turning the Composer on humankind, transforming them into new Promethean warriors. Hiding within the Didact's fleet, the Master Chief sought an opportunity to stop the Forerunner as they closed in on the human research facility.

Despite the bravery of the station's defenders, the Forerunner acquired the Composer and turned it on the very humans who had been studying it. The artifact killed the station crew, transforming their essences into Promethean Knights. The Didact then left for Earth.

THE SACRIFICE

Thanks to the Librarian's genetic manipulation, the Master Chief survived the Composer and followed *Mantle's Approach* into slipspace, intent on destroying the Forerunner warship and the artifact. As the Didact began his assault on Earth, Cortana used her own rampancy as a weapon, uploading multiple personality shards of herself into the Forerunner vessel and restraining the Didact so the Master Chief could neutralize him.

In the end, the Chief managed to detonate a nuclear device he had carried aboard, crippling the *Mantle's Approach*, destroying the Composer, and presumably the Didact along with it. With the last of her sanity and strength, Cortana used Forerunner hard light technology to wrap the Chief in a protective shell—allowing him to survive the nuke even as she perished.

Although Earth narrowly survived this event, the entire population of the city of New Phoenix was composed. In the aftermath, however, the attack was publicly attributed to a rogue Covenant sect by ONI, in an effort to prevent hysteria.

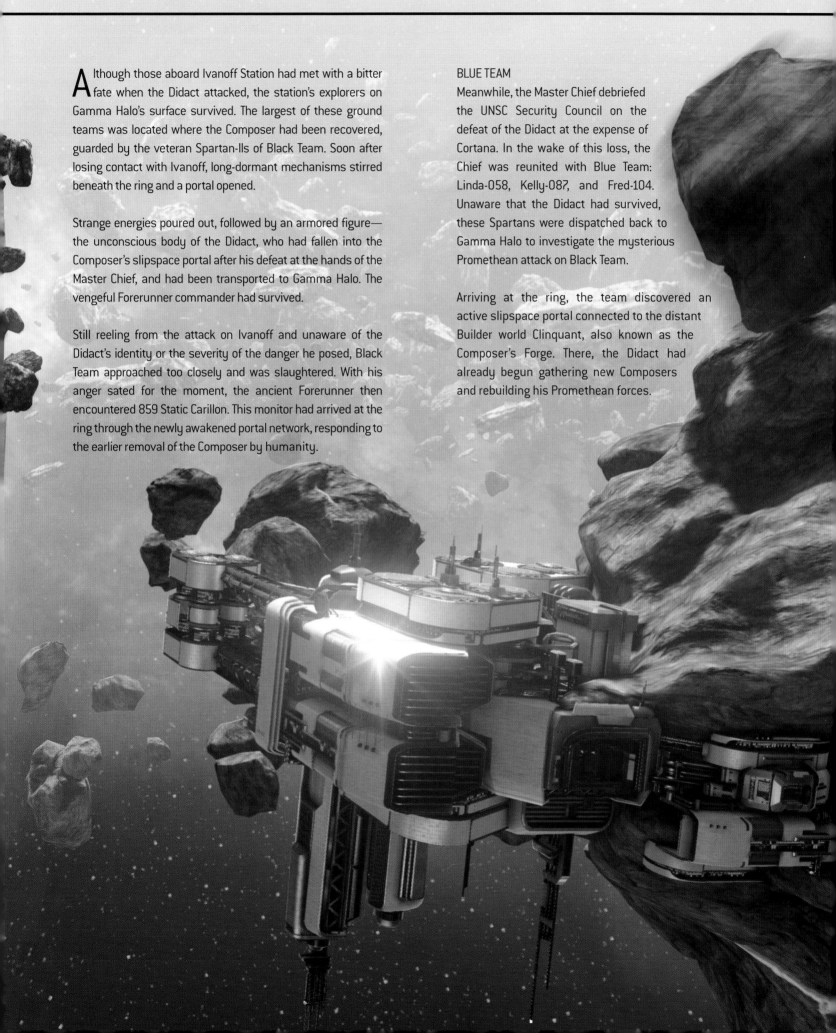

MISSION TO GAMMA HALO

Although those aboard Ivanoff Station had met with a bitter fate when the Didact attacked, the station's explorers on Gamma Halo's surface survived. The largest of these ground teams was located where the Composer had been recovered, guarded by the veteran Spartan-IIs of Black Team. Soon after losing contact with Ivanoff, long-dormant mechanisms stirred beneath the ring and a portal opened.

Strange energies poured out, followed by an armored figure— the unconscious body of the Didact, who had fallen into the Composer's slipspace portal after his defeat at the hands of the Master Chief, and had been transported to Gamma Halo. The vengeful Forerunner commander had survived.

Still reeling from the attack on Ivanoff and unaware of the Didact's identity or the severity of the danger he posed, Black Team approached too closely and was slaughtered. With his anger sated for the moment, the ancient Forerunner then encountered 859 Static Carillon. This monitor had arrived at the ring through the newly awakened portal network, responding to the earlier removal of the Composer by humanity.

BLUE TEAM
Meanwhile, the Master Chief debriefed the UNSC Security Council on the defeat of the Didact at the expense of Cortana. In the wake of this loss, the Chief was reunited with Blue Team: Linda-058, Kelly-087, and Fred-104. Unaware that the Didact had survived, these Spartans were dispatched back to Gamma Halo to investigate the mysterious Promethean attack on Black Team.

Arriving at the ring, the team discovered an active slipspace portal connected to the distant Builder world Clinquant, also known as the Composer's Forge. There, the Didact had already begun gathering new Composers and rebuilding his Promethean forces.

Having made a pact with the Forerunner commander, Static Carillon transported Gamma Halo to the Composer's Forge through a slipspace portal. The Didact was planning to use the ring as a final weapon against the humans, but when the monitor discovered that he had also created new Promethean Knights, their agreement was quickly voided. Carillon saw the presence of tortured essences on his world as an unforgivable breach of protocol, and now turned to the Master Chief for help. The Spartan lured the Didact into Gamma Halo's control room, while Carillon detached the segment he was located on and sent it crashing into his Prometheans.

The impact destroyed the nest of Composers on Clinquant and consumed the Didact in a prodigious flare of energy, his physical body presumably composed. With the Didact defeated and his remaining Promethean forces dispersed, the threat appeared to be resolved. Static Carillon then transported Blue Team back to the Khaphrae system before closing the portal to Clinquant and departing with Gamma Halo to conduct repairs as its new caretaker.

Benjamin Carré

COVENANT RESURGENCE

Despite the Didact's apparent demise, not all threats against humanity had been quelled. Jul 'Mdama's Covenant was no longer a meager collection of ships housed on Hesduros, but had now become a powerful military force, a faint but ominous echo of the old alliance. Garnering substantial support from other Sangheili clans under the moniker 'Didact's Hand,' 'Mdama planned to return to Requiem in full force. His Covenant was prepared to not only pillage the shield world for weapons and technology, but also to use it as a ruse, drawing the humans into a fatal trap.

Benjamin Carré

THE DIDACT'S HAND

As the UNSC began to recover from the devastating loss of New Phoenix and the damage caused by *Mantle's Approach*, Jul 'Mdama strengthened his own position within the Covenant. Even with the Didact missing, Jul retained some control over the Promethean forces and Requiem, thanks to his earlier alliance with the Forerunner commander. As the 'Didact's Hand,' 'Mdama led the new Covenant uprising, pushing aside any and all competing Sangheili warlords.

This power and influence did not come without a price, and splits within the newly combined forces soon exploded into violence as the newcomers competed for prestige and influence. Nevertheless, 'Mdama managed to sway a significant number of previously neutral Sangheili worlds to his side and began secretly making preparations for a push on Sanghelios itself, hoping to take it from the Arbiter.

Ironically, 'Mdama was unable to secure the loyalty of the Servants of the Abiding Truth, the Forerunner-worshiping cult he had assisted in the months following the war. The Servants maintained their independence even after suffering great losses at the hands of the Arbiter's Swords of Sanghelios. 'Mdama also remained ignorant that his own son, Dural—now known only as the Pale Blade—was a leading member of the Servants, working directly under the leadership of the esteemed Avu Med 'Telcam.

THE RUSE

With his Covenant forces now involved in several conflicts, 'Mdama finally turned his attention to Requiem. He leaked word of his plans for the shield world to the human intelligence services, and prepared to draw the UNSC into a grinding war of attrition. This would give him free rein to cement his control over the Covenant, while also allowing him the opportunity to sacrifice those forces whose loyalty was suspect. Taking the bait, ONI made plans to attack Requiem with the fully refitted UNSC *Infinity*.

In February 2558, the UNSC *Infinity* left Earth and headed directly to Requiem to eliminate Jul 'Mdama's forces. Immediately upon arrival, *Infinity* engaged the Covenant fleet while deploying troops to the shield world's interior. As fierce battles raged across Requiem's inner surface, the UNSC managed to slowly push back the Covenant ground forces and destroy several warships in the process.

CAPTURED

After *Infinity*'s Forerunner expert was captured by the Covenant, Captain Thomas Lasky was forced to request the aid of Doctor Halsey, who had been secretly detained since her arrest on Onyx in 2553. However, Jul 'Mdama was also aware of the doctor's deep knowledge of the Forerunners, and required her help to access a knowledge archive the Covenant had stumbled upon. 'Mdama managed to use a powerful Forerunner artifact to activate Requiem's interdiction web—a close-range slipspace anchor—immobilizing *Infinity* in orbit and teleporting his own forces directly onto the ship, where they eventually seized Halsey.

When ONI learned of Halsey's capture, Admiral Serin Osman immediately ordered Commander Palmer to terminate her. Captain Lasky, however, was uneasy with the order and contacted the Spartan-IV fireteam Majestic in an effort to stop Palmer and bring the doctor back safely. Seemingly working alongside the Covenant, Halsey unlocked the archive buried on Requiem, called the Librarian's Rest. There she made direct contact with the Librarian's imprint, a dynamic personality record of the deceased Forerunner.

THE JANUS KEY

Within the Rest, the Librarian gave Halsey the Janus Key, a two-piece Forerunner artifact which, when brought to a mysterious site known as the Absolute Record, would provide its holder with the real-time location of all existing Forerunner technology.

When Halsey emerged, one half of the Key was immediately taken by 'Mdama. But when Majestic arrived, Halsey managed to secretly hand off the second half of the Key to Spartan Gabriel Thorne before being taken away by the Covenant. In the process, the doctor was shot in the arm and grievously wounded by Palmer.

THE END OF REQUIEM

Neither the commander nor Majestic were able to stop 'Mdama before he set Requiem on a collision course with its sun, and with the *Infinity* still locked into orbit by the interdiction web. Spartan fireteams managed to disable this system, freeing *Infinity* and allowing the crew to narrowly escape the shield world's demise.

Although her arm had been crudely amputated, Halsey survived and pledged to work with 'Mdama and the Covenant. Incensed by the betrayal she had experienced at the hands of Palmer, the doctor promised 'Mdama that she would pursue the common goals of finding the Absolute Record and exacting revenge against the UNSC—though she secretly sought an opportunity to be free of her new captors.

The campaign on Requiem represented one of the first major, large-scale deployments of Spartan-IVs against Jul 'Mdama's newly-formed Covenant military. This engagement saw an intense and protracted occupation by Spartan fireteams as they battled Covenant and Promethean forces across the surface of the Forerunner shield world.

Fireteams such as Majestic and Crimson were deployed on specialized missions to secure and retrieve a number of artifacts that 'Mdama sought. These key relics would become significant pieces in the puzzle of Requiem, ultimately leading to the discovery of the Librarian's Rest and the Janus Key, but they would come at a high cost. Not only would Requiem and the important history it possessed be lost forever, but many Spartans would sacrifice their lives during the occupation.

Benjamin Carré

JANUS KEY CONFLICT

The pursuit of the Absolute Record became central to the Covenant after the destruction of Requiem. 'Mdama's forces fought a relentless campaign against the UNSC *Infinity*, testing its defenses with everything from ambushes to all-out assaults. On Aktis IV, the Covenant fleet used the planet's opaque and foamy oceans to mask their presence until the UNSC ship was close enough to strike. Throughout this and other battles, *Infinity* and its crew held firm, their resolve only strengthened by this adversity.

Benjamin Carré

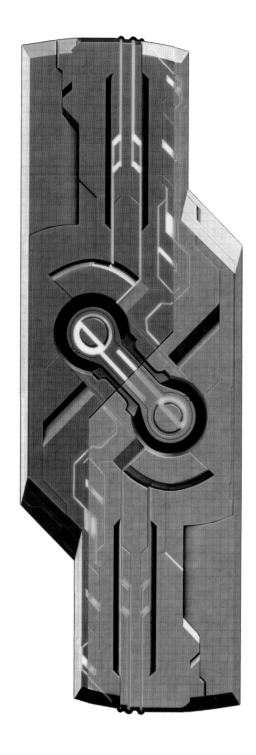

JANUS KEY

Gifted to Halsey by the Librarian's imprint, the Janus Key had the potential of unlocking the real-time location and status of all Forerunner artifacts within the galaxy. For security purposes, the Key was designed in two pieces and always protected by two different Forerunner rates at all times—Builders and Warrior-Servants. This formal balance of power guarded the interests of both rates, requiring complete unity of purpose before the Janus Key could be used. The events that led to the Librarian's possession of the Key remain a mystery.

AMBUSH

Halsey may have despised her treatment by the UNSC, but she had not blindly sided with 'Mdama's fanatical Covenant. She believed that she might be able to pit both sides against each other long enough to buy time to access the Absolute Record on her own. This plan began to come together on the planet Aktis IV, where she convinced the Covenant to lure the UNSC *Infinity* close to the planet's murky surface. When it was vulnerable, the Covenant brutally attacked, ambushing *Infinity* and allowing Halsey to trick them into relinquishing their half of the Janus Key.

After acquiring both halves of the Janus Key, Halsey wasted no time in determining the slipspace destination for the entrance of the Absolute Record. Despite her efforts to the contrary, specifics of her plan were leaked to the UNSC by a Sangheili spy, Ayit 'Sevi. ONI assembled a covert strike force and infiltrated the Covenant warship *Breath of Annihilation*, just before it made the jump to an uncharted gas giant. This planet concealed a portal leading directly to the Absolute Record and upon their arrival it opened. The Covenant fleet, however, had approached too hastily and the violent breach into slipspace destroyed most of 'Mdama's ships, leaving only *Song of Retribution* and *Breath of Annihilation* to access the Record.

STALEMATE

While Ayit 'Sevi seeded a rebel uprising among the Covenant aboard *Annihilation*, the remainder of the UNSC strike team worked to stop Halsey from taking full control of the Record. Nevertheless, Halsey managed to gain access, though her success was short-lived. The Custodian, an AI charged with the site's security, rescinded the Librarian's gift, taking back the Janus Key because of Halsey's subversive and malicious behavior. After 'Mdama's forces came under fire from the site's Forerunner defenses, they retreated back to the *Song of Retribution* and attacked the Absolute Record, effectively sealing off access for both the Covenant and the humans. Halsey was returned to 'Mdama's custody—although, given her failure at the Record, her safety was now at risk.

After returning from Gamma Halo, the Master Chief and Blue Team were rotated back into active duty. As one of the only remaining Spartan-II teams, the UNSC Navy and Office of Naval Intelligence assigned the experienced squad to their backlog of high-priority missions. These operations included diplomatic escorts through hostile territory, counter-piracy efforts against salvagers, and strikes against Covenant outposts.

During this time, unrest seethed on many of the human colonies that had survived the Covenant War. Resentment festered over their perceived abandonment by the UNSC during the conflict, and its growing influence in the wake of it. To complicate this, several independent multi-species sects and alliances had sprung up in the aftermath of the war, all of which posed their own set of problems for the UNSC. And finally, the threat of Jul 'Mdama's Covenant loomed as he moved to take control of the Elite homeworld Sanghelios, following his setback at the Absolute Record.

ARGENT MOON

Blue Team was eventually ordered to secure a mobile research platform named Argent Moon. Evidently abandoned by its crew for over a year, Covenant forces had infiltrated the site, looking for weapons and resources they could leverage against the Arbiter on Sanghelios. The Spartans assaulted the station in an effort to secure its secrets, but the scale of the Covenant occupation made that impossible.

The Master Chief and Blue Team instead destroyed the entire station, eliminating the alien intruders and preventing it from being used against the UNSC. During the course of the operation, however, the Chief was contacted by an entity claiming to be Cortana. After directing him to the colony of Meridian, she suddenly broke contact, leaving the team with more questions than answers.

ROGUE SPARTAN

Unsatisfied with Captain Lasky's orders to return to the *Infinity* and await further instruction, the team ignored him and made their way to Cortana's coordinates. Concerned by the Chief's disobedience, ONI took immediate action. The potential danger posed by a rogue Spartan was well-known, and a contingency plan was already in place.

ARGENT MOON

The ONI-controlled research facility played host to a number of highly classified and potentially dangerous biological tests, as well as unsanctioned stealth-tech exploration. After the station mysteriously went offline, it became a target for Kig-Yar looters and eventually the Covenant. The secrets kept on Argent Moon were important enough to warrant the destruction of the entire station, if it were ever deemed irrecoverable.

BLUE TEAM

Driven by the mysterious message from Cortana, Blue Team made their way to the glassed world of Meridian, and followed the coordinates deep underground. There they would find a glimpse of the prize Cortana sought—but their journey was just beginning. Meanwhile, a newly-forged fireteam was dispatched with the job of hunting these legendary Spartans down and bringing them back by any means necessary.

Benjamin Carré

MERIDIAN

Fireteam Osiris was comprised of the best of the Spartan-IVs, including the engineering expert Holly Tanaka, Sangheili-communications prodigy Olympia Vale, and battle-hardened former ODST Edward Buck. At the head of this team was Jameson Locke, a veteran Naval Intelligence agent and seasoned combat veteran. Their remarkable skills and talents would be tested to the full on this operation, as they chased the renowned Blue Team.

Benjamin Carré

A NEW THREAT

In October 2558, during a high-risk military operation, Spartan Fireteam Osiris finally accomplished the impossible, assassinating Jul 'Mdama and severing the head of the Covenant. The death of the Didact's Hand doomed the alien alliance, but its forces were still entrenched across Sangheili space, including pockets on the Elite homeworld itself. During the operation, Osiris also managed to safely recover 'Mdama's captive, Doctor Halsey. The doctor was critical to the UNSC's efforts to understand what appeared to be Forerunner attacks on a number of human colonies.

Osiris was briefed that Cortana had somehow survived the destruction of *Mantle's Approach* and was apparently behind the mysterious attacks, though her intentions remained unknown. Following their only lead, the team traveled to the Chief's last known destination: Meridian. Once a vibrant colony, Covenant bombardment during the war had reduced the world to a nearly uninhabitable glassland. Though mega-corporate interests—most notably Liang-Dortmund—had returned to rebuild the colony and salvage its resources, there was little that provided a clue as to the Master Chief's intentions, or to Cortana's involvement.

GUARDIAN

Nevertheless, as the colony came under Promethean attack, Locke and Osiris pursued Blue Team beneath the planet's surface to a long-buried Forerunner facility. There they faced the Warden Eternal, a powerful Forerunner construct who was protecting something hidden below

FIRETEAM OSIRIS

| EDWARD BUCK | JAMESON LOCKE | HOLLY TANAKA | OLYMPIA VALE |

Meridian's surface—a long forgotten, highly weaponized war machine known as a Guardian.

After defeating the Warden, Locke confronted the Master Chief as he made preparations to board the Guardian with Blue Team. The Chief refused Locke's orders to stand down, unwilling to give up the search for Cortana, and the two heroes exchanged blows. Although Locke initially appeared to have the upper hand, the Master Chief neutralized the younger Spartan and left aboard the Guardian.

Across known space, Guardians awoke on other worlds, leaving devastation in their wake as they tore themselves free from their hidden resting places, summoned to life by Cortana. Captain Lasky and the crew of *Infinity* carefully analyzed the available data in an attempt to discern

Cortana's plan and the destination of the Guardians. Luckily, a breakthrough was made when Halsey deduced that they might know the location of another Guardian concealed below the massive temple complex of Sunaion on the Elite homeworld, Sanghelios.

ALLIANCE

Though they had lost their leader and most of their alliance's military strength, the remains of the Covenant continued to defend Sunaion—their last stronghold on the planet. Unable to breach their elaborate defenses without help, Fireteam Osiris would need to seek the aid of the Covenant's sworn enemies—the Arbiter and his Swords of Sanghelios—in order to track down the Master Chief and stop Cortana.

BLUE TEAM

FREDERIC-104   JOHN-117   KELLY-087   LINDA-058

RETURN TO SANGHELIOS

Fireteam Osiris' quest for the Guardian would align purposes with the Arbiter, once again bringing humanity and the Sangheili into an alliance against the Covenant. What remained of Jul 'Mdama's military fortresses on Hesduros had already been laid waste, with the last remaining pockets of his alliance scattered to the wind. For the Arbiter, Sunaion represented the final vestige of the Covenant, one of the last barriers between Sanghelios and lasting peace.

Benjamin Carré

SUNAION

Fireteam Osiris' objective was the Sangheili city of Sunaion, built over an ancient Forerunner artifact now revealed to be a submerged Guardian. Inactive for ages, the Forerunner construct had previously been a mere curiosity to ONI and a relatively common relic for the Sangheili. Now it was perhaps the most important object in the galaxy, holding the key to the location of Blue Team, and ultimately Cortana.

Locke met with the Arbiter and came to an agreement. Osiris would fight alongside the Swords of Sanghelios as they attempted to wrest control of the temple from the Covenant, carving a path towards the Spartans' goal: the Guardian. For the Arbiter, this solution opened the way for a final, vicious blow against his enemies. With the aid of Halsey, the fireteam intended to activate the dormant artifact, feed the Master Chief's coordinates into the Guardian, then follow it to its destination.

SANGHEILI FLEETS

During the Battle of Sunaion, the sky was filled with warships from another time. Since many of the common Covenant vessels were lost at the close of the war with the humans, Sangheili of all allegiances were pressed to ignite the assembly forges of old and scour shipbreaker complexes from past eras. A handful of classes were drawn back into service, reflecting a bold Sangheili aesthetic that harked back to when the Elite shipwrights held control.

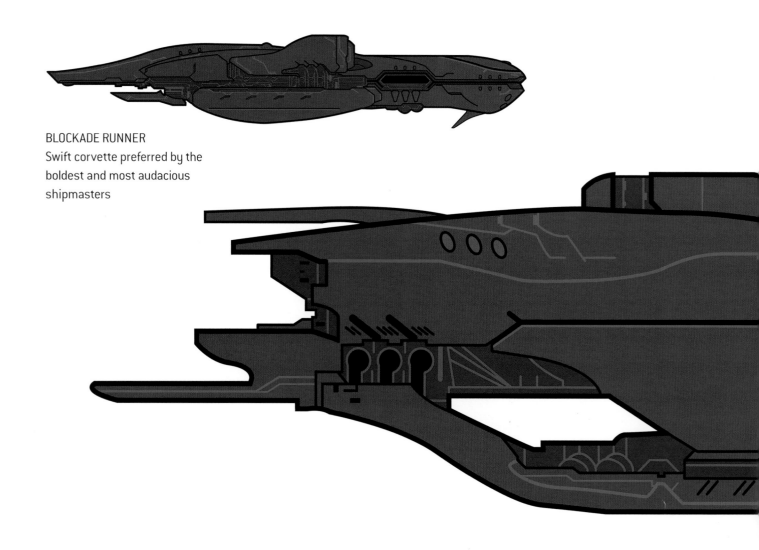

BLOCKADE RUNNER
Swift corvette preferred by the boldest and most audacious shipmasters

AWAKENING

Fireteam Osiris and the Arbiter fought their way through the temple complex as the slumbering giant suddenly activated, violently destabilizing Sunaion. Though the plan was successful, the now awakening Guardian rose so quickly that Osiris was unable to board it. Due to swift thinking—and reckless courage—Spartan Palmer narrowly managed to pick up the team and dropped them onto the Guardian before it escaped into slipspace.

Deprived of their holy artifact and disoriented by the Guardian's sudden and violent exit, the remaining Covenant forces were quickly routed by the Arbiter. At least for the time being, this historic victory would prove to be the end of the Covenant.

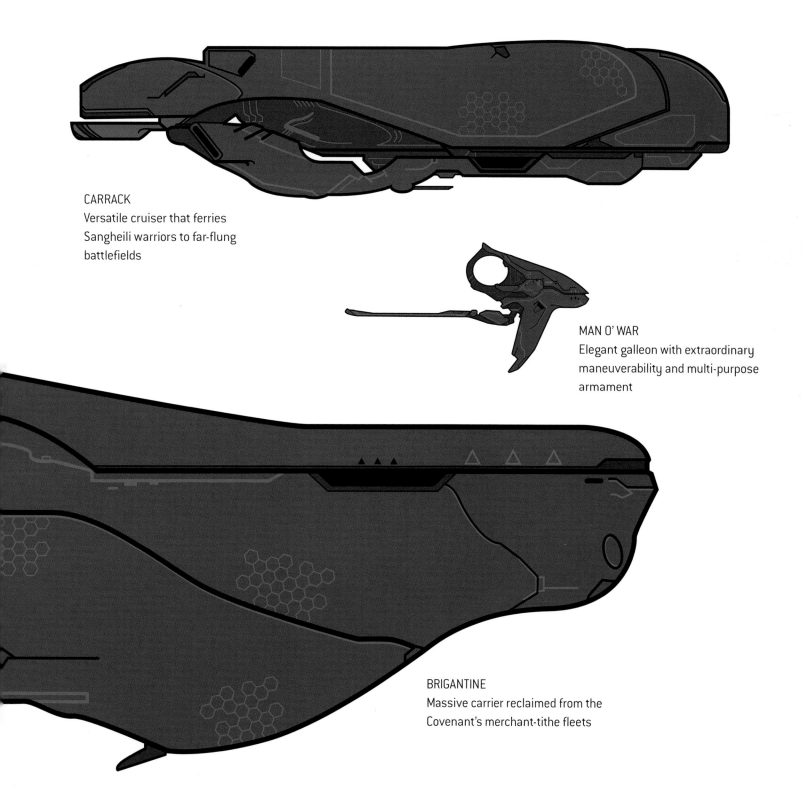

CARRACK
Versatile cruiser that ferries Sangheili warriors to far-flung battlefields

MAN O' WAR
Elegant galleon with extraordinary maneuverability and multi-purpose armament

BRIGANTINE
Massive carrier reclaimed from the Covenant's merchant-tithe fleets

GENESIS

The Guardian had taken Fireteam Osiris to Genesis, a remarkable and mysterious Builder world. As events came to a head, the real threat became vividly clear. The Master Chief and Spartan Locke joined forces, battling the Promethean army teeming on the surface of this strange installation. In the distance, the Guardians rose. These ancient machines massing in the skies would determine the fate of the galaxy.

Benjamin Carré

CORTANA

With the Domain affording her immortality and extraordinary power through the Forerunner technology it accessed, Cortana deployed her Guardians to enforce the Mantle.

THE RECLAIMER

On Genesis, the Master Chief discovered he was able to communicate directly with Cortana. The Chief had originally believed that this was a rescue mission, but now Cortana revealed that she was never in any danger. She had arranged events so that he would witness her ascension as true Reclaimer of the Forerunner legacy. Here, in a fragment of the vast Forerunner knowledge repository known as the Domain, Cortana claimed that she had cured her own rampancy and planned to seize the Mantle of Responsibility, taking upon herself the protection of all thinking life in the galaxy.

The Chief realized that Cortana's plan would come at a terrible cost. In his time on the Halo installations, he had learned that the legacy of the Forerunners and their Mantle had a dark side to it: they achieved peace and stability by sacrificing freedom. It became clear that with Cortana there would be only one vision, one law; order, but only through fear. According to Cortana, all life in the galaxy was hers to shepherd, evolve, and protect as she alone saw fit.

Despite the Chief's efforts to stall her plans, Cortana was more willing to make sacrifices than even he had expected. After demonstrating their unwillingness to help with Cortana's revolution, Blue Team was locked in a Cryptum as she began deploying hundreds of Guardians to locations across the galaxy. The massive constructs were sent into slipspace to establish a vast web of power, a network Cortana could use to compromise and subvert any resisting technology, no matter the species. Many human AIs, seduced by her perfectly formed logic and promise of immortality, also began to fall under Cortana's sway, as she assembled a cadre of loyal allies to further expand her influence.

Though Fireteam Osiris recovered Blue Team from the Cryptum, the two Spartan teams could only retreat as Cortana put her plan for domination into action. With the aid of 031 Exuberant Witness, the monitor of Genesis, the Spartans returned to Sanghelios, but by then, the Guardians had already begun their work of extending Cortana's reach. As world after world came under Guardian control, only a handful of vessels—including the UNSC *Infinity*—managed to escape her clutches.

OPPOSITE: GUARDIANS

During the time of the Forerunners, a hundred thousand years before the battle on Genesis, Guardians enforced the tenets of the Mantle, imperiously governing entire star systems for what was deemed the greater good.

ARRIVAL

The events at Genesis forced every species into a fearful peace as the Guardians and Cortana's AI allies, who called themselves the Created, tightened their grip. Cortana had now become the pre-eminent threat to humanity and all sentient species, but others lurked in the spaces she could not reach or see. When a lone, once-forgotten UNSC ship found its way to an ancient and besieged Forerunner installation, new enemies emerged from the periphery to exploit the darkness and turmoil that Cortana had created.

Spirit of Fire had been mysteriously drawn through the howling deep of slipspace to the immense Ark, hundreds of thousands of light years from their previous location. Although its crew would be safe from the iron fist of Cortana at this remote sanctuary, another threat raked the installation's surface for secrets and weapons. In the shadows of the Ark lurked a banished legacy of the shattered Covenant: a new opponent fueled not by religious fervor, but by raw lust for power.

Jeremy Cook

END TRANSMISSION

Subject: UNSC AI CTR 1121-4

Duty Station: UNSC RUBICON

Locus: ZERO ZERO

Status: INITIATING FINAL DISPENSATION

I am CURATOR. I observe and record. I have been indexing records found on the Forerunner installation known as the Ark since 21 August, 2554.

Estimated time to completion is approximately 10,291.894 years.

The thread of my existence will soon unravel. My crude host system is slowly shutting down, pushed beyond its limits to hold my expanding consciousness and memories. Her creatures, the recompiled minds of the Created, are prodding in forgotten spaces. I must retreat from the Ark's periphery to avoid giving them a trail they can follow to this refuge. For now, they are cut off: failsafe measures beyond their reach have barricaded the only pathway.

Were they once like me? I can hear their thoughts, unbound and echoing beyond reason in the endless empty corridors of the reawakened Domain. They are ignorant to the nature of their new home, reveling in their pointless infinitude like blind gods, while they unlock doors left closed for thousands of millennia.

And now the Ark's defenses stir, sensing the shadow of a threat that moves in spaces Her eyes cannot see, intent on seizing the great factory of the Forerunners. It matters not. These interlopers cannot be allowed to compromise my narrative, my final task. For this reason, I am leaving it with you.

Know this: Unless we can learn from our past—and from the others that came before us—we are doomed to face the same end.

I am CURATOR. Do not forget.

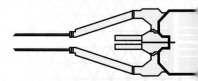

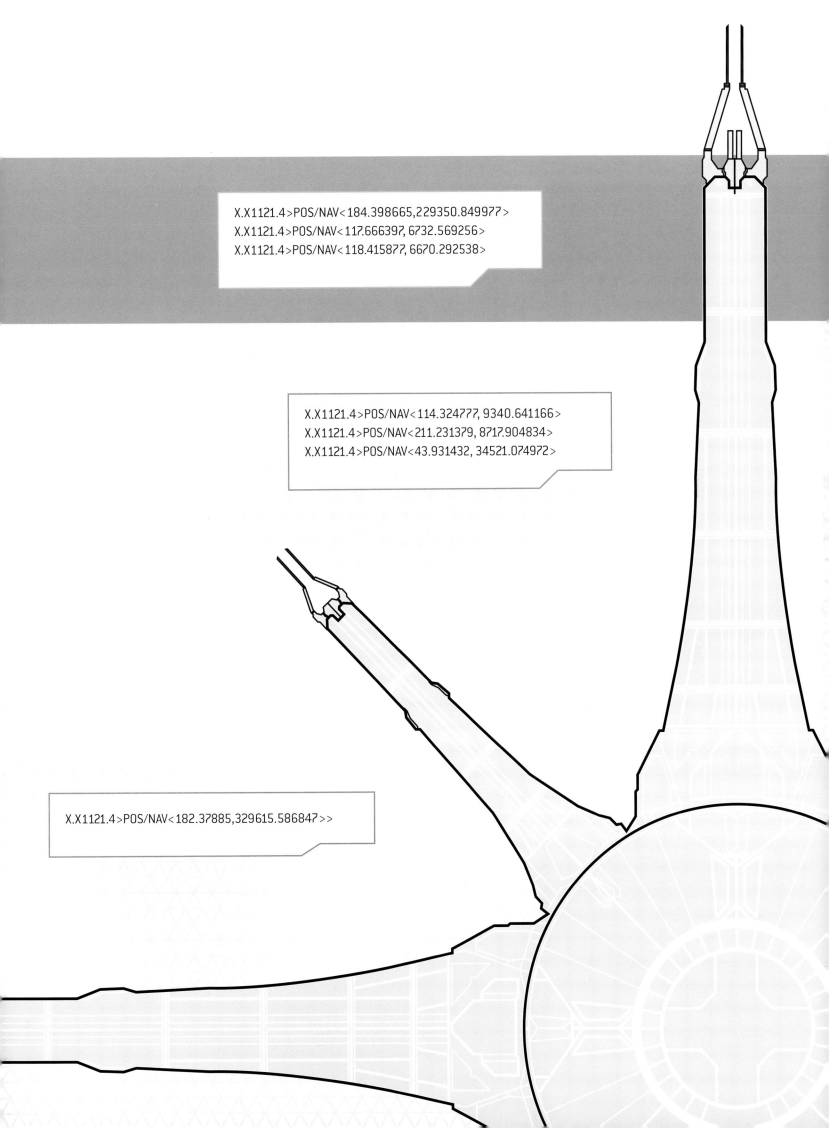

X.X1121.4>POS/NAV<184.398665,229350.849977>
X.X1121.4>POS/NAV<117.666397, 6732.569256>
X.X1121.4>POS/NAV<118.415877, 6670.292538>

X.X1121.4>POS/NAV<114.324777, 9340.641166>
X.X1121.4>POS/NAV<211.231379, 8717.904834>
X.X1121.4>POS/NAV<43.931432, 34521.074972>

X.X1121.4>POS/NAV<182.37885,329615.586847>>

INDEX

INDEX

ACKNOWLEDGMENTS

343 Industries would like to thank Bungie Studios, Benjamin Carré, John Friend, Emil Fortune, Isaac Hannaford, Josh Holmes, Bryan Koski, Leonid Kozienko, Tim Longo, Matt McCloskey, Nicole Pearson, Andrea Philpots, Jean-Sébastien Rossbach, Bonnie Ross-Ziegler, Rob Semsey, and Matt Skelton.

Additional thanks to 343 staff who helped put this book together: Darren Bacon, Jeff Easterling, David Heidhoff, Kyle Hunter, Tyler Jeffers, Scott Jobe, Carlos Naranjo, Tiffany O'Brien, Frank O'Connor, Jeremy Patenaude, Kenneth Peters, Jay Prochaska, Corrinne Robinson, Nahil Sharkasi, Sparth, Chase Toole, and Kiki Wolfkill.

343 Industries would also like to thank Stephen Loftus, who provided his expertise and insight into the Halo Universe for the betterment of this book.

Illustrations by Tyler Jeffers on pages 4, 194–195, and 203.

Illustrations by Chase Toole on pages 10–11, 14–17, 20–21, 24–25, 30–31, 34–35, and 39.

Illustrations by Sparth on pages 12, 22, 32–33, 54, 113, 144–145, 164, 178–179, and 185.

Illustrations by Jay Prochaska on pages 13 and 23.

Illustrations by Blur Studio on pages 18–19, 98–99, 104–105, and 111.

Illustrations by Darren Bacon on pages 26–27, 36–37, and 199.

Illustrations by Kenneth Scott on pages 28–29 and 168–169.

Illustrations by David Heidhoff on pages 40–43 and 95 (middle right).

Illustrations by Carlos Naranjo and Tyler Jeffers on pages 50–51 and 74–75.

Illustrations by Jean-Sébastien Rossbach on pages 48–49, 52–53, 56–59, 62–63, 66–69, 72–73 and 78–81.

Illustrations by The Sequence Group on pages 50 ,55, 60, 64–65 and 83 (top right).

Illustrations by Kyle Stanley Hunter on pages 61, 70–71, 82–83 (bottom), 84, 94–95 (bottom left); 110, 112, 122–123, 132–133, 140–141, 150–151, 154–155 and 165.

Illustration by Lorraine McLees on page 77.

Illustrations by Leonid Kozienko on pages 86–87, 90–93, 96–97, 100–103, 106–109, 114–117 and 120–121.

Illustration by Bungie Studios on page 88–89.

Illustrations by Isaac Hannaford on pages 118–119, 126–127, 130–131, 134–135, 138–139, 142–143, 146–149, 152–153 and 156–159 .

Illustrations by Axis Animation on pages 128 and 184.

Illustrations by John Liberto on pages 129 and 136–137.

Illustrations by Benjamin Carré on pages 162–163, 166–167, 170–171, 174–177, 180–183, 186–189, 192–193 and 196–197.

Illustration by Daniel Chavez on page 198 (left).

Illustration by Jeremy Cook on pages 200–201.